Contents

Phonemic Awareness

Learning to Know

Trace and color the picture. What is it?

Aa

Objectives: Initial

Mathematical Thinking

Learning to Know

Color the patterns.

Objectives: Color a simple pattern.

Trace lines from left to right.

Developmental Writing

Learning to Know

Objectives: Trace lines.

Draw a picture of yourself.

Artistic Expression and Appreciation

Learning to Be

This is me!

Objectives: Draw their own face.

Color the things you use in the morning.

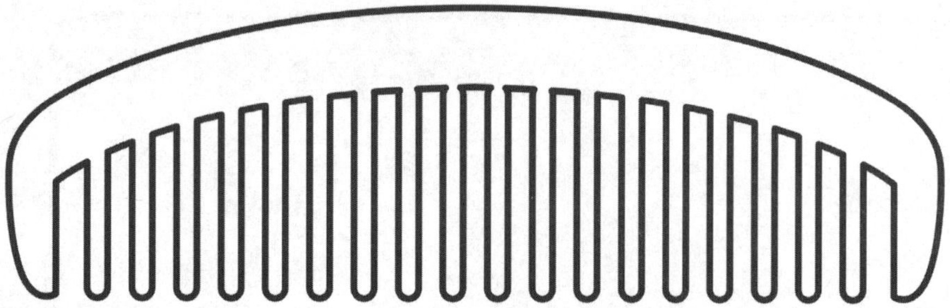

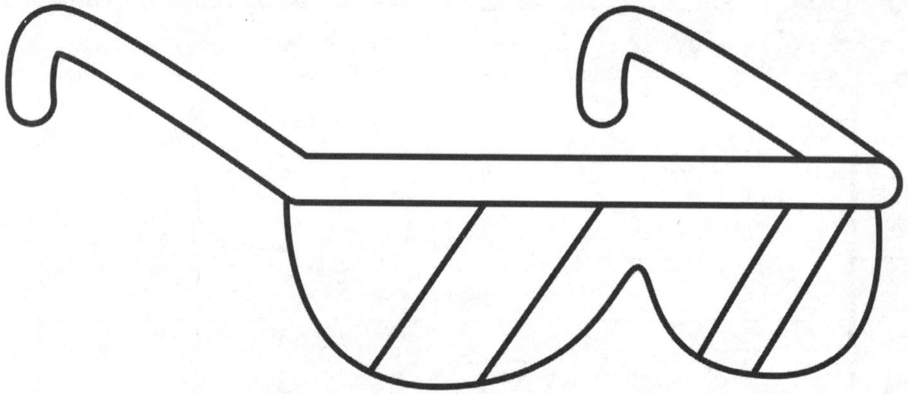

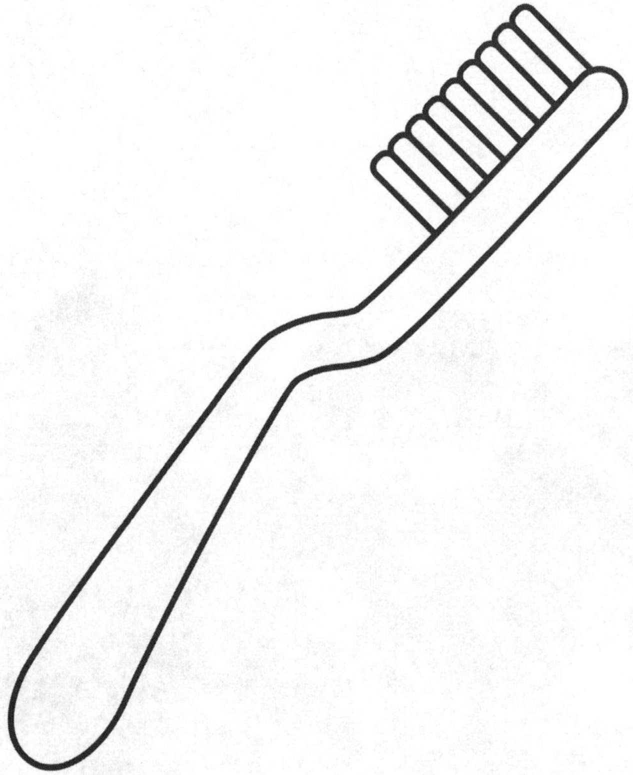

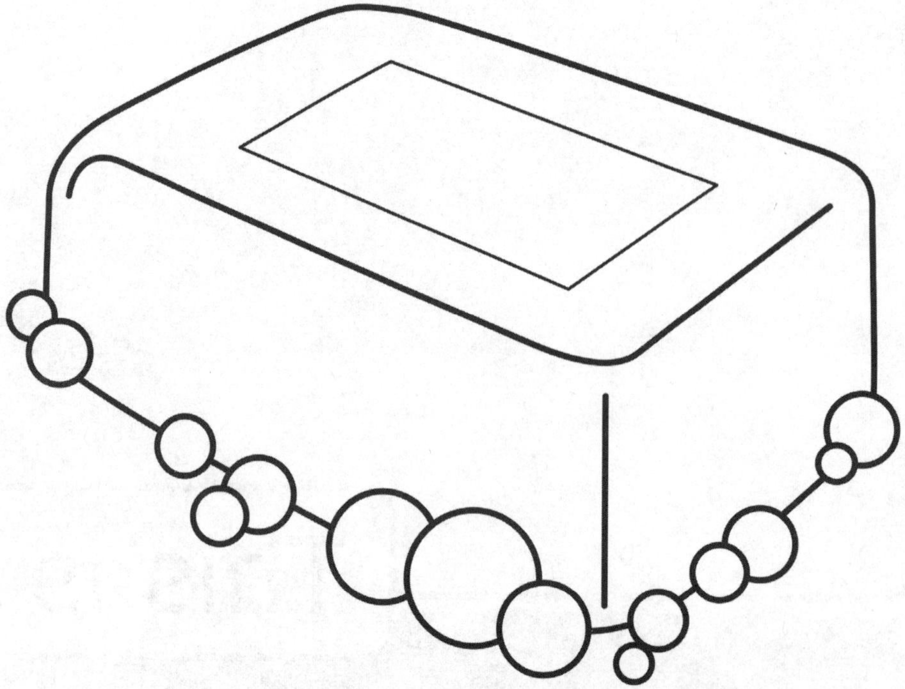

Objectives: Personal hygiene.

Trace the circle to make an *a*.
Then, circle all the same letters.

Phonemic Awareness

Learning to Know

A a

A a A

a

a A

A a

a

a

a

A

A

a a a

Objectives: Initial short /*a*/ sound.

Color big squares.

Mathematical Thinking

Learning to Know

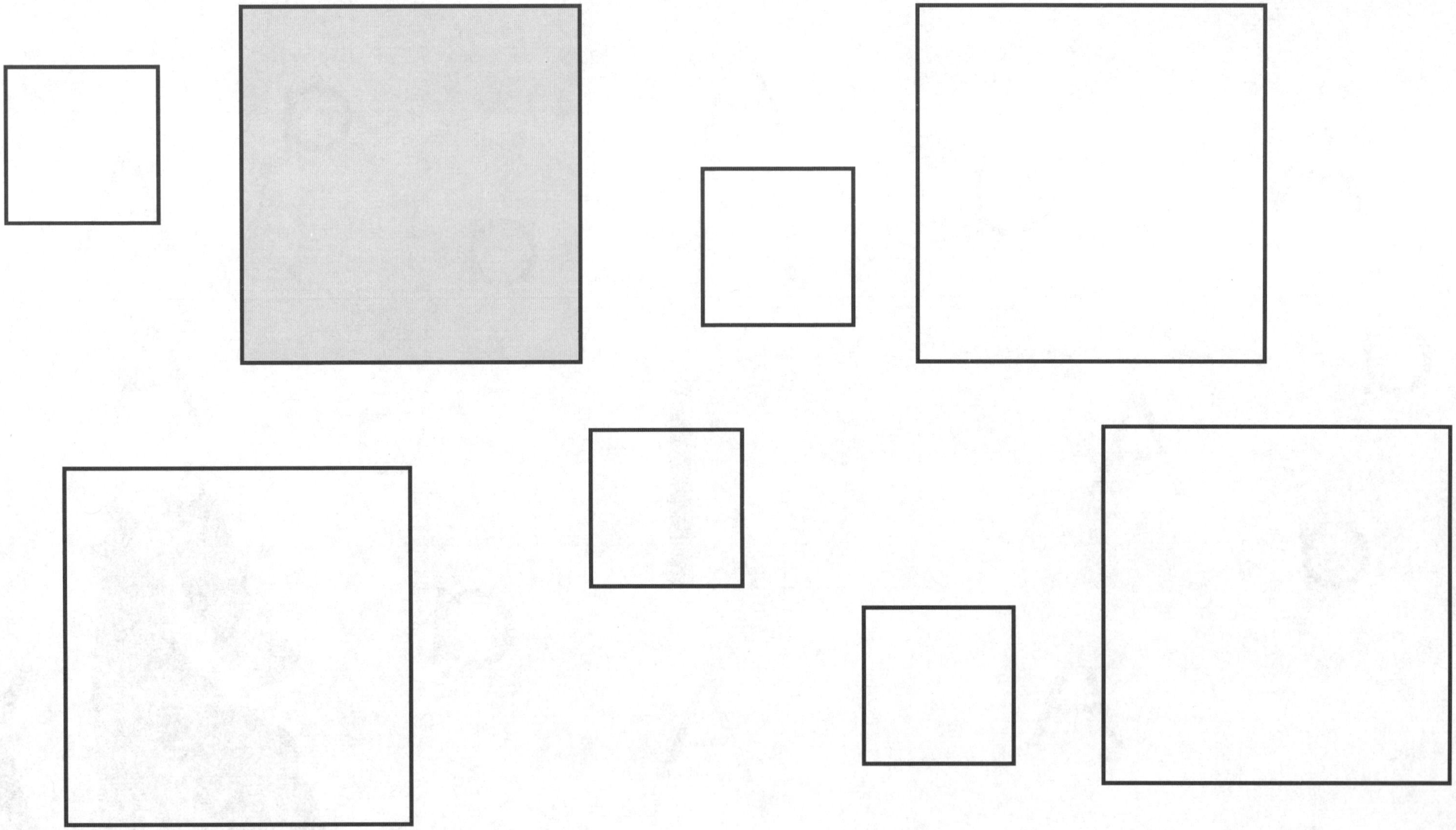

Objectives: Identify big shapes.

Paste string on the letter and the apple.

a

Objectives: Circles. Letter *a*.

Artistic Expression and Appreciation

Learning to Be

How do you feel today? Draw your face.

Objectives: Express emotions/feelings.

Match the columns.

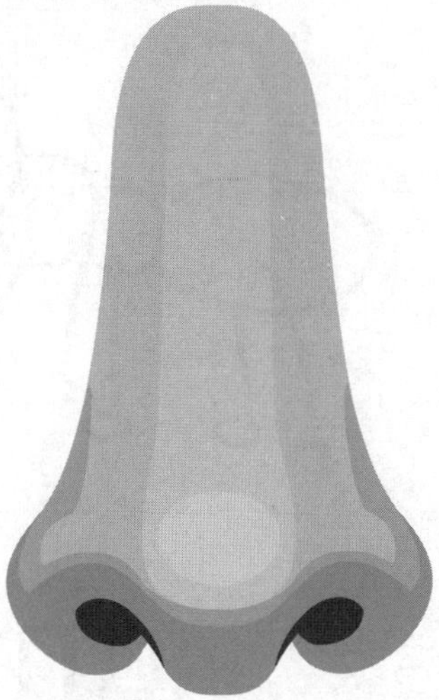

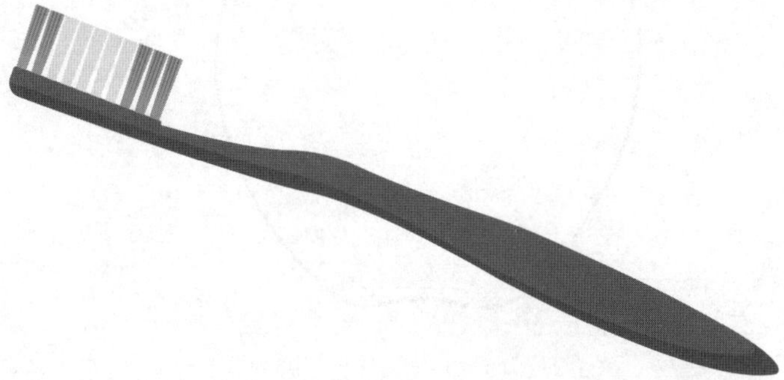

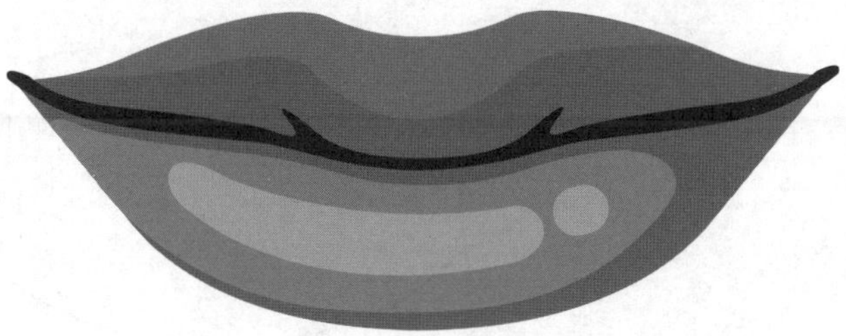

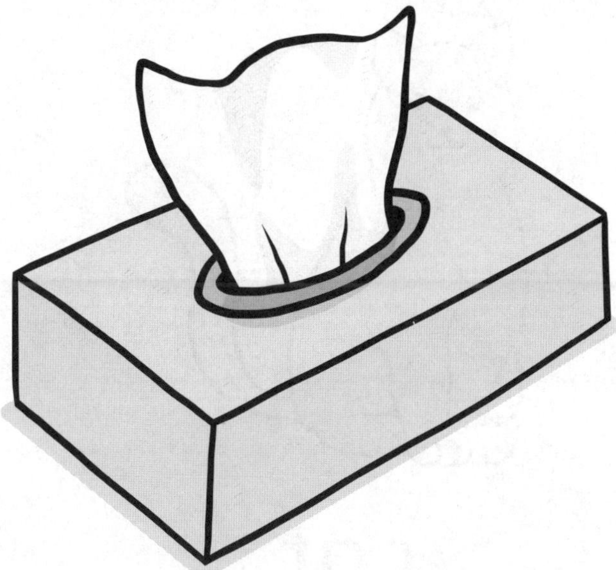

Objectives: Personal hygiene.

Circle the *a*'s and color the animals.

Phonemic Awareness

Learning to Know

apple

ant

a

cat

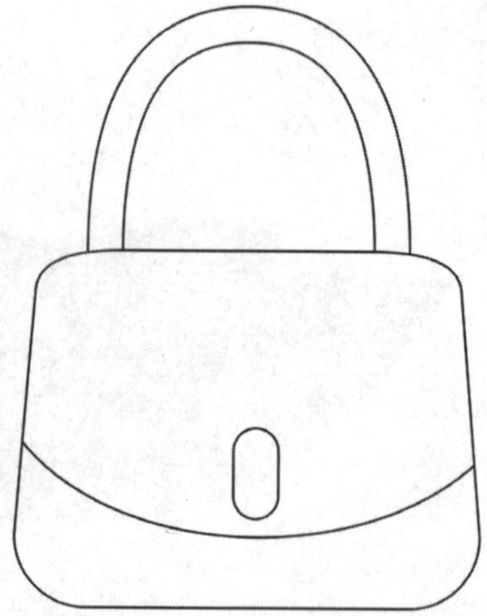

bag

Objectives: Initial and middle short /a/ sound.

Mathematical Thinking

Learning to Know

Trace the numbers and color the school objects. Match them.

3

1

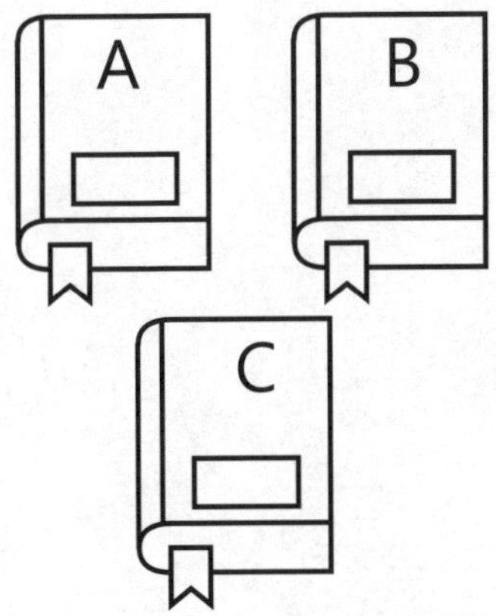

2

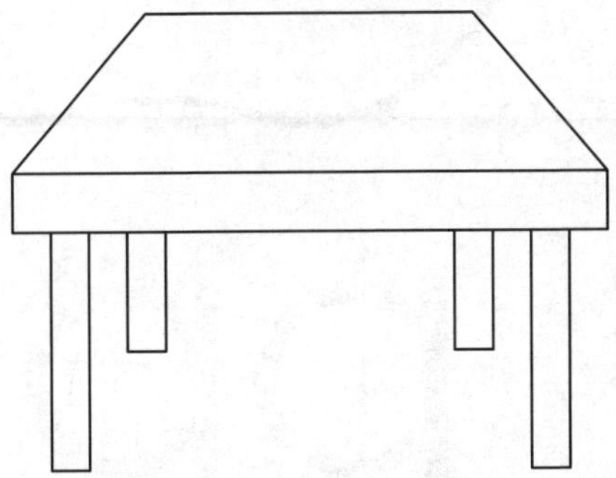

Objectives: Match sets of objects to the corresponding number.

- **Trace the missing letter. Paste red or green paper on the apple.**

Developmental Writing

Learning to Know

apple

ant

Objectives: Circle, letter *a*.

- **Draw a girl on page 1.**
  Draw a boy on page 2.

Artistic Expression and Appreciation

Learning to Be

Objectives: Identify boy and girl.

Complete the pictures. Decorate the page with paper balls.

Artistic Expression and Appreciation

Learning to Be

Objectives: Faces.

Color the pictures.
Circle the big *A*'s.

Big Al

Small Anne

Objectives: Initial short /a/ sound.

Mathematical Thinking

Learning to Know

Cut from a magazine and paste.

BIG

small

Objectives: Begin to sort objects.

Read and trace the letters. Use different colors.

Developmental Writing

Learning to Know

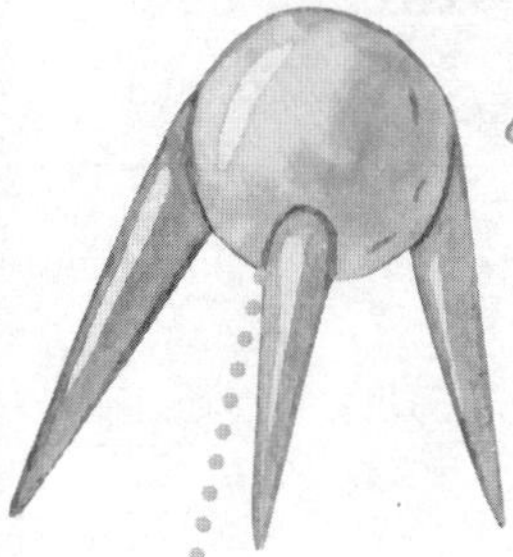

A A A A

a a a a

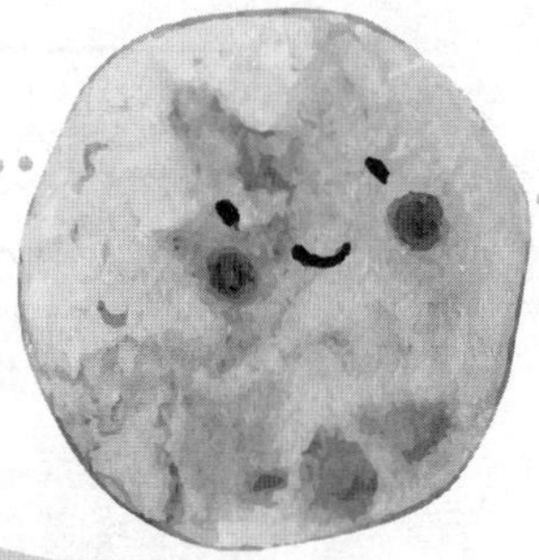

Objectives: Letter *Aa*.

Color the pictures. Use finger paint.

Artistic Expression and Appreciation

Learning to Be

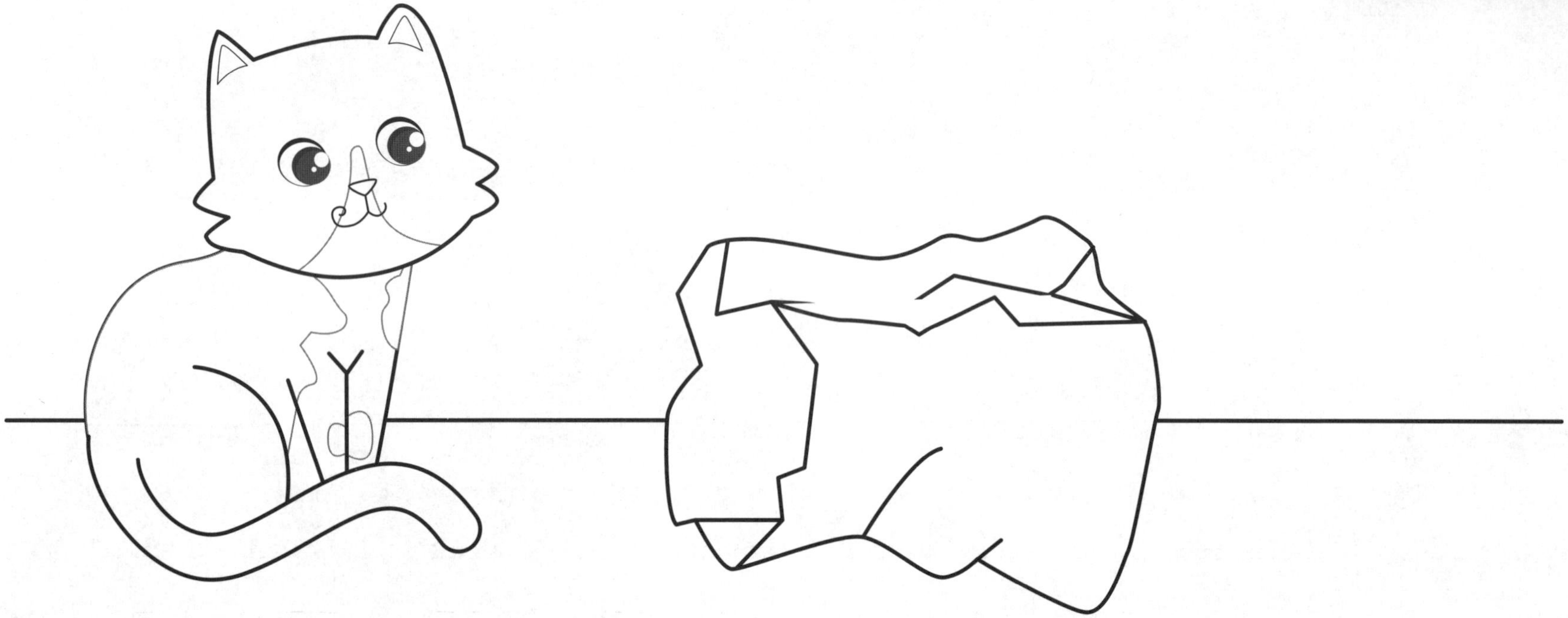

Objectives: Letter *a*.

Color what you use to wash your hands.

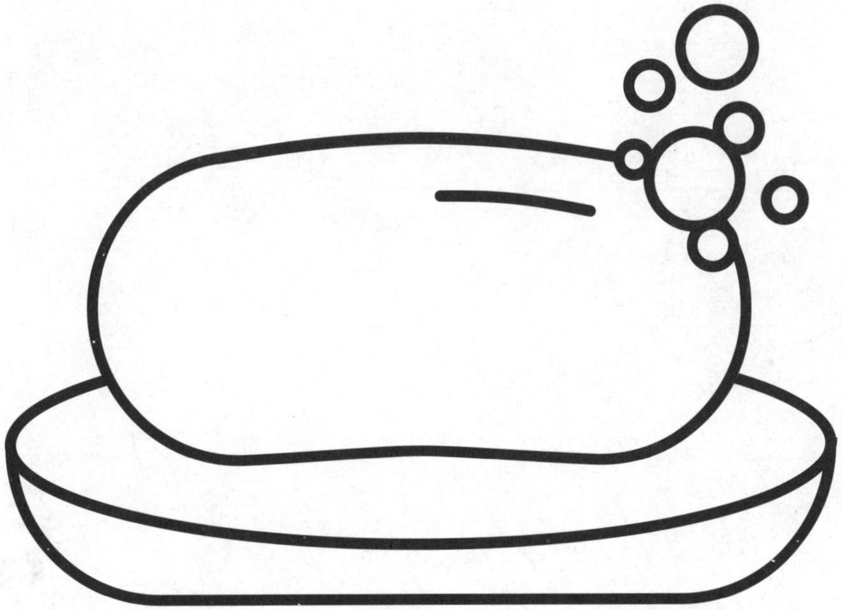

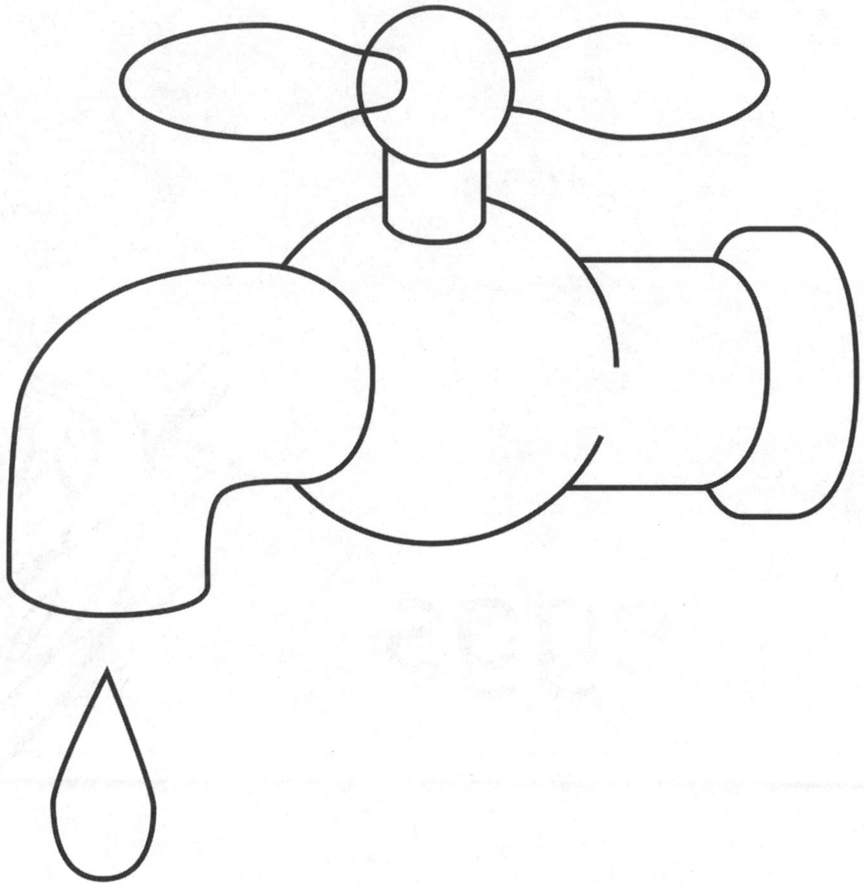

Objectives: Personal hygiene.

Trace and color the eggs.

e

eggs

Objectives: Short /e/ sound.

Finish the pattern.

Mathematical Thinking
Learning to Know

Objectives: Follow a simple pattern.

Trace the letters. Color the nest. Decorate the egg.

Developmental Writing

Learning to Know

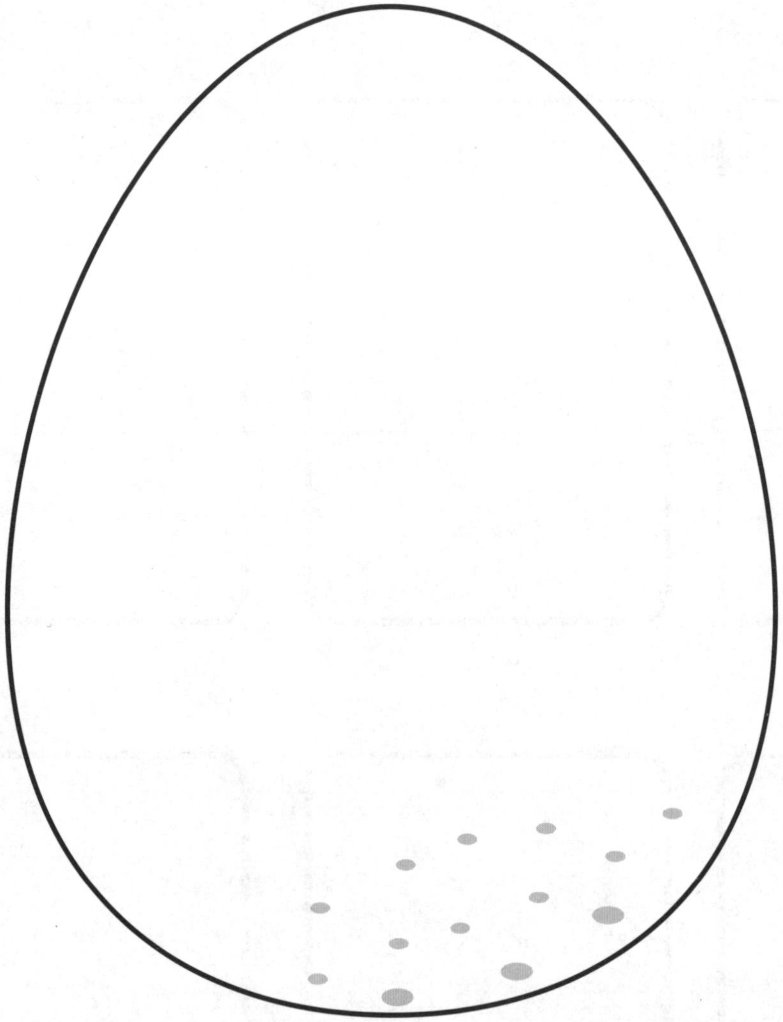

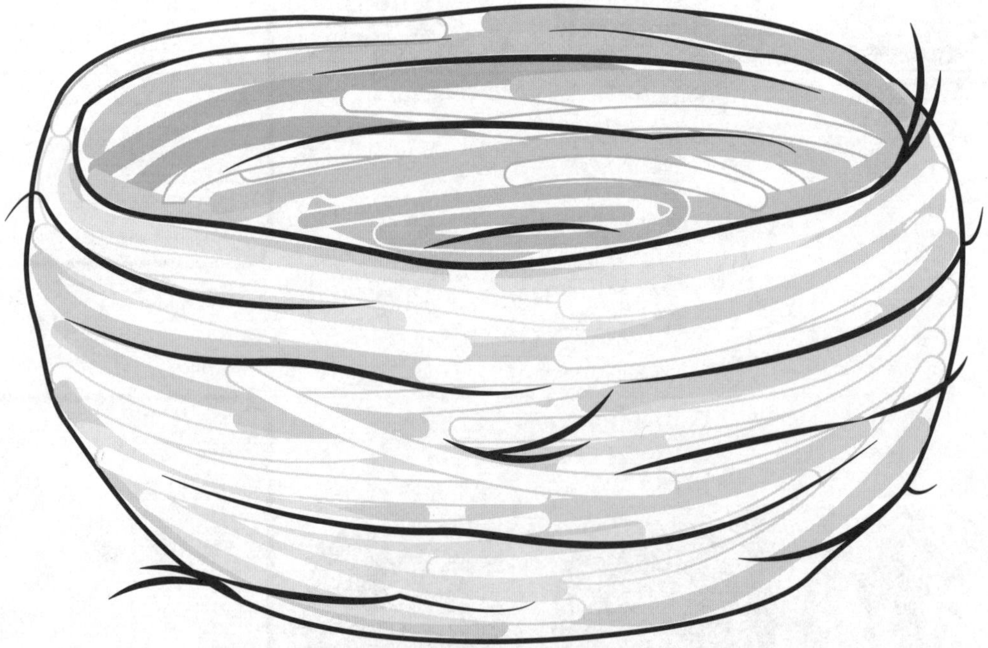

Egg

Nest

Objectives: Letter *Ee*.

Artistic Expression and Appreciation

Learning to Be

Color and match the pictures.

Objectives: Symmetry in the body.

Draw a box around how you feel today and color the picture.

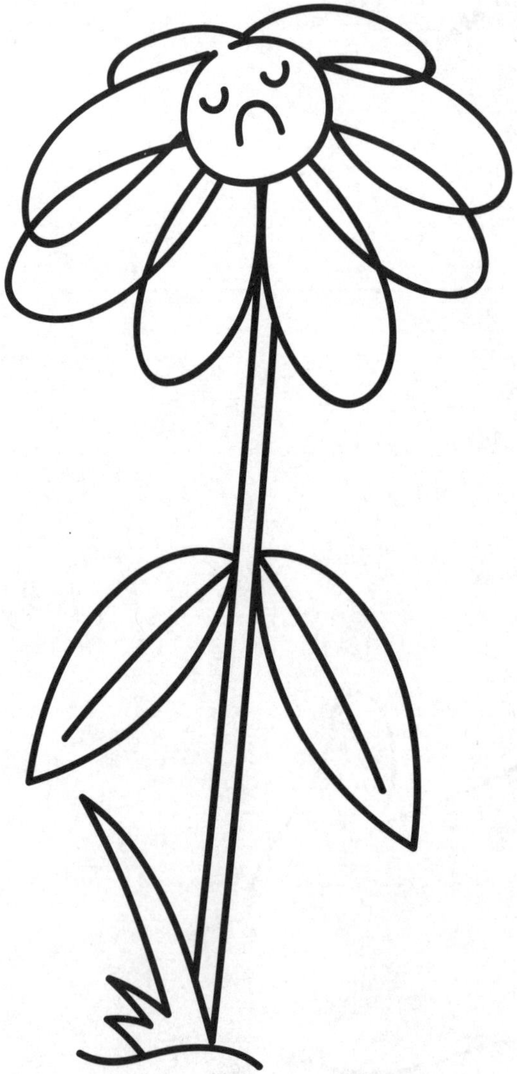

Objectives: Express emotions/feelings.

Phonemic Awareness

Learning to Know

Color and match the pictures. Circle the letter e.

egg

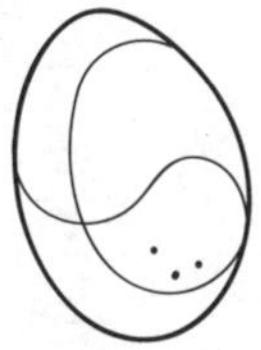

hen

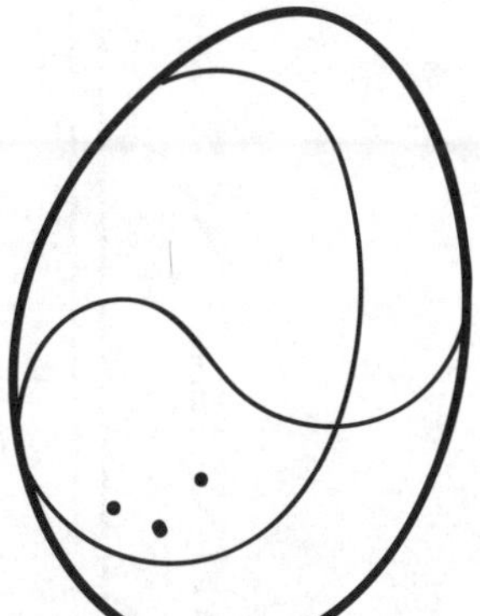

Objectives: Short /e/ sound.

Trace the numbers. Draw 1, 2, and 3 objects.

Mathematical Thinking

Learning to Know

1

2

3

Objectives: Trace and identify numbers.

Trace and paste yarn on the letters.

Developmental Writing

Learning to Know

Ee

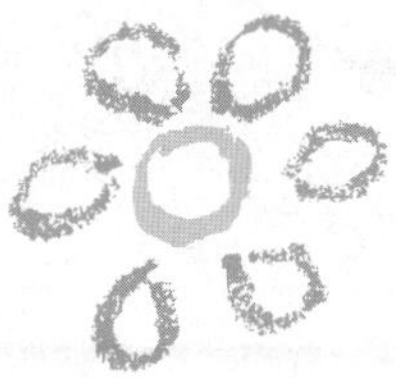

Trace the letters with your finger.

Objectives: Letter *Ee*.

Color the parts you have one of.

Exploration and Knowing of the World

Learning to Do

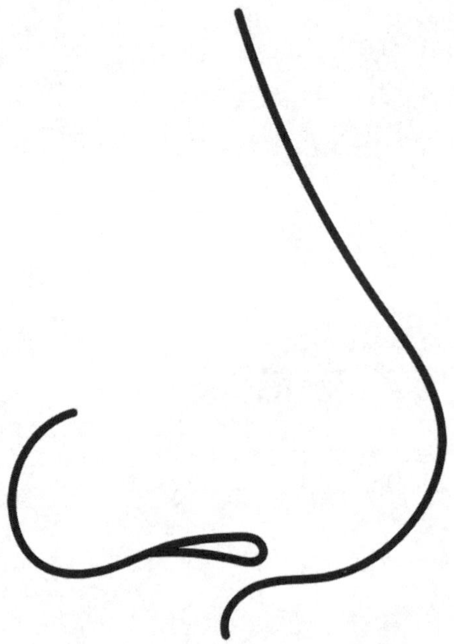

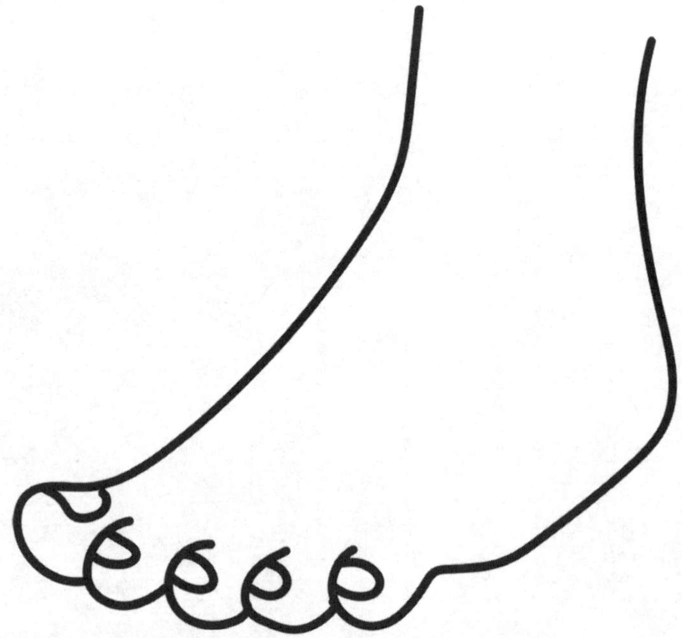

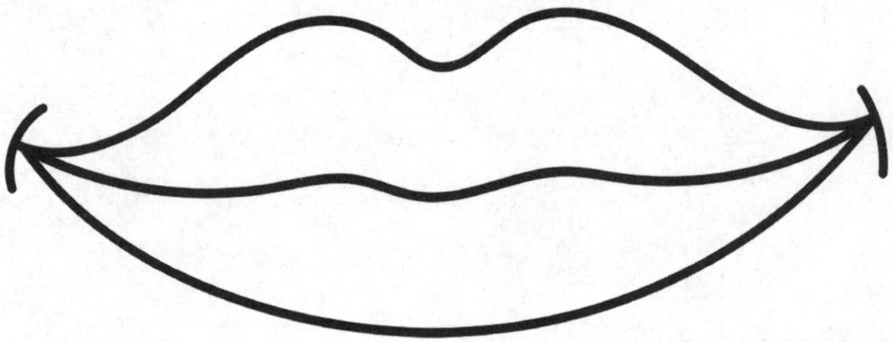

Objectives: Symmetry in the body.

Exploration and Knowing of the World

Learning to Do

Trace the lines of things that go in the pencil bag.

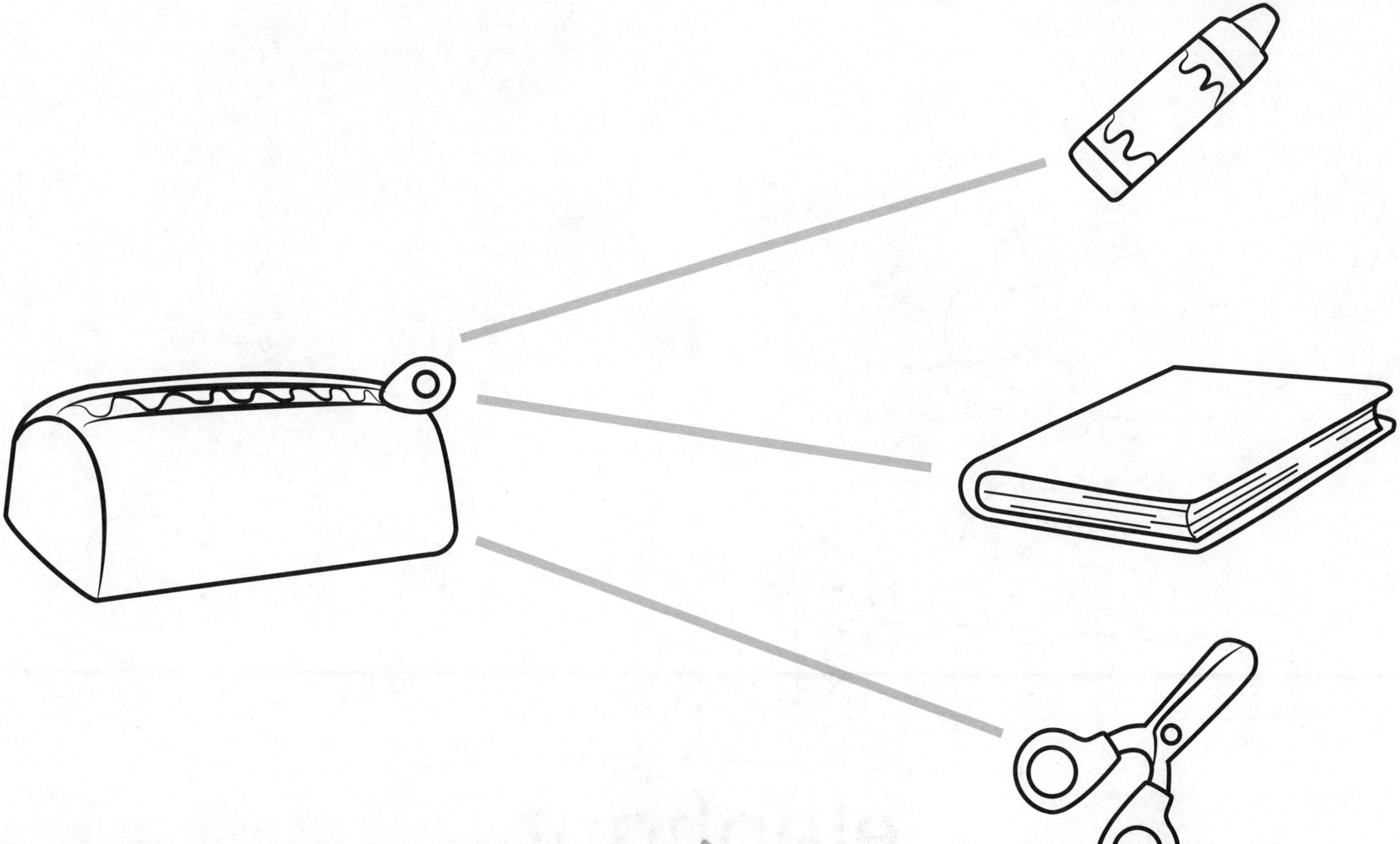

Color the things you have.

Complete the picture.

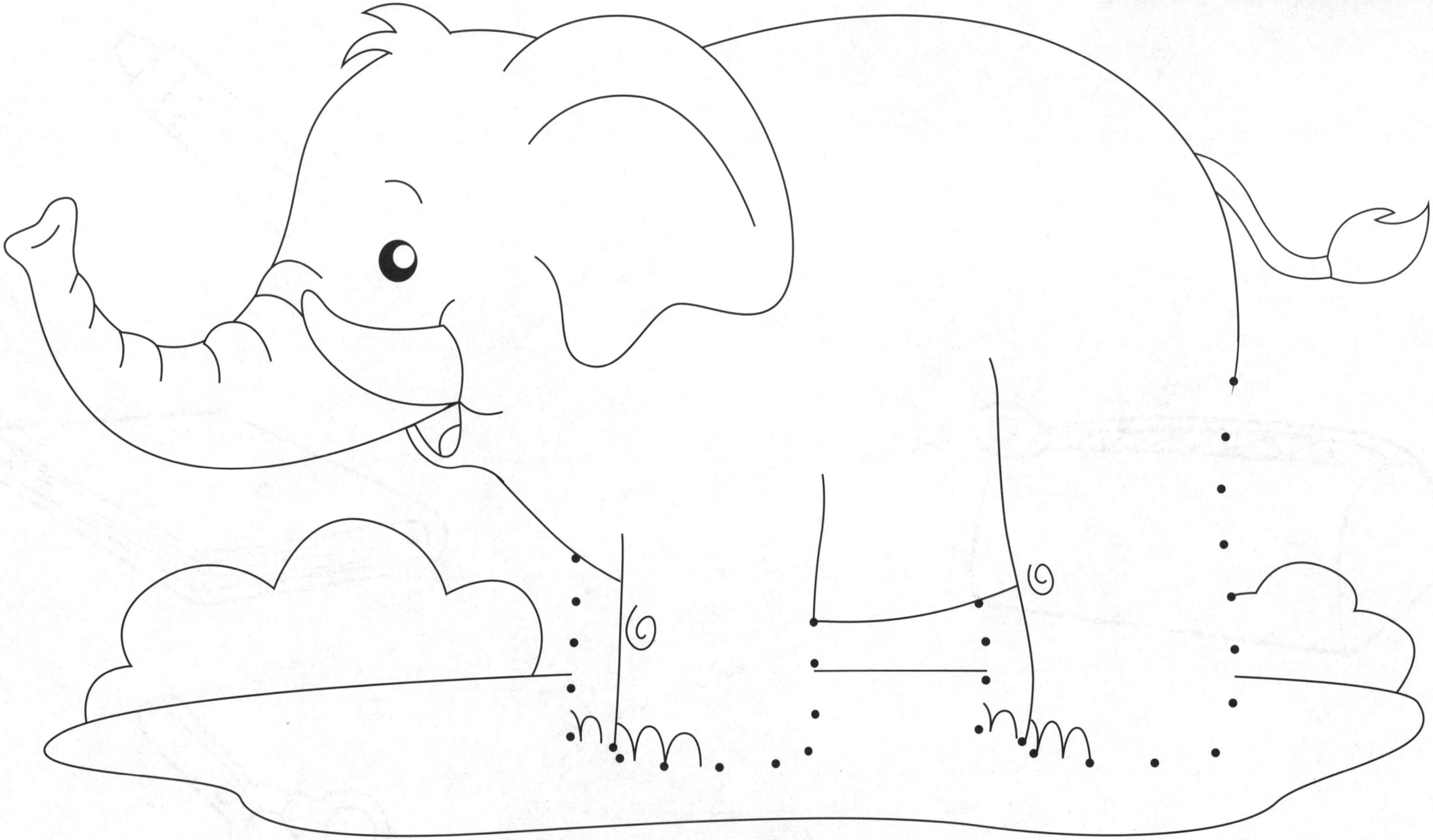

elephant

Objectives: Short /e/ sound.

Paste paper on big. Cross out small.

Mathematical Thinking

Learning to Know

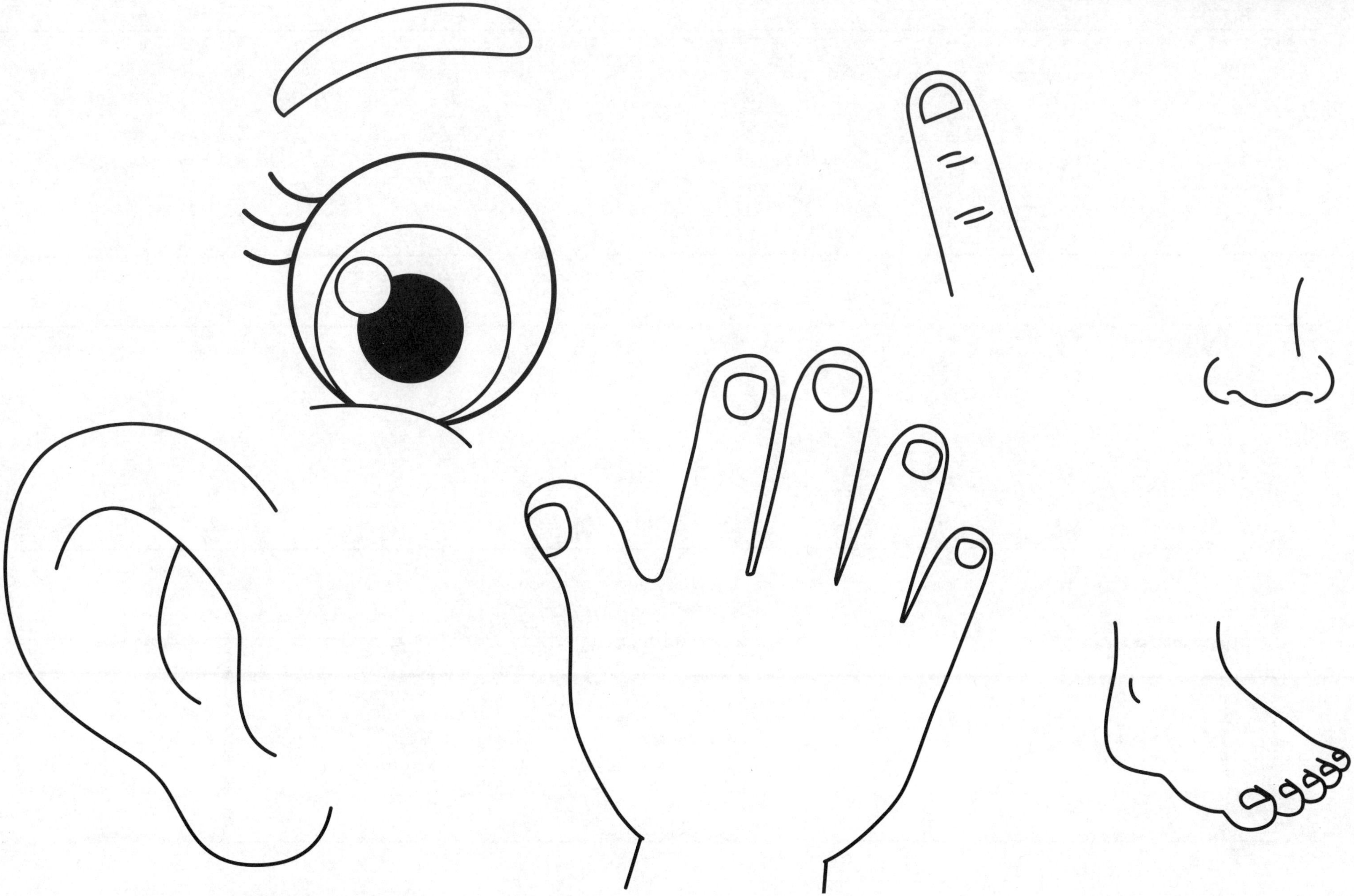

Objectives: Identify big and small.

Trace the lines and connect the dots with different colors.

Developmental Writing

Learning to Know

Objectives: Line letter *Ee*.

Cut on the line. Finger paint what you cut with.

Artistic Expression and Appreciation

Learning to Be

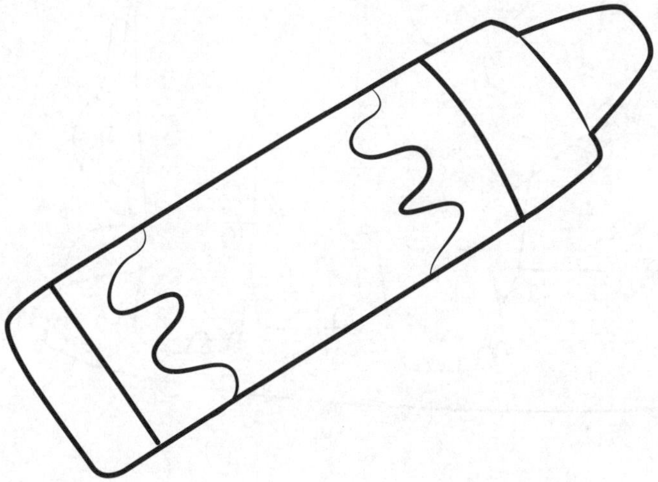

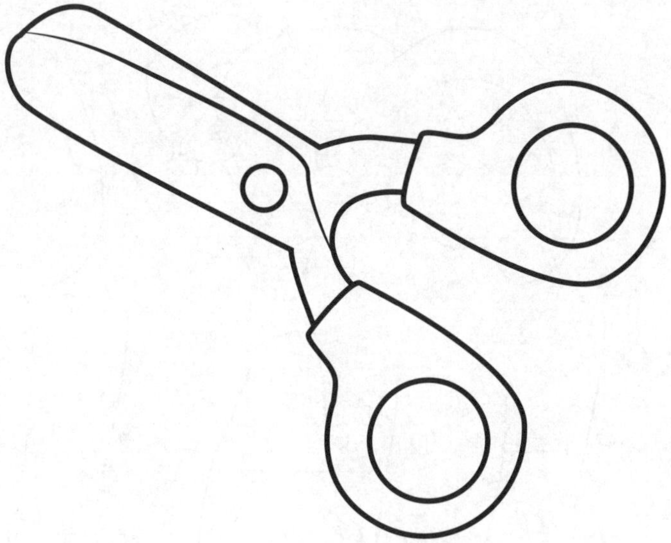

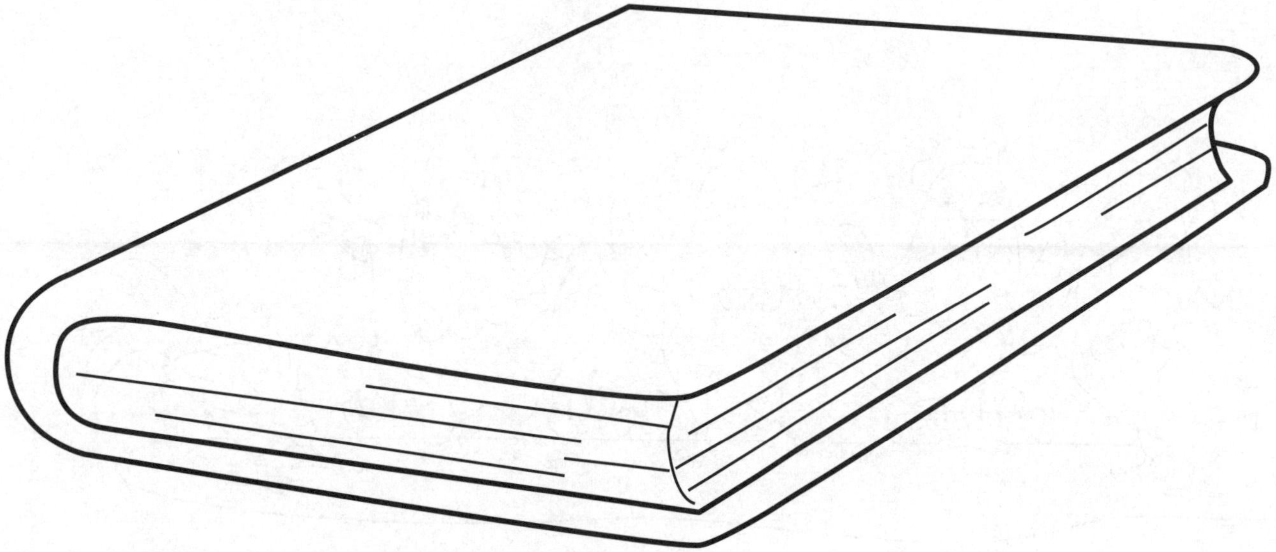

Objectives: Everyday school objects and what they are for.

Color the sad one in each line.

Personal, Social, and Emotional Development

Learning to Live Together
Learning to Live with Others

Objectives: Express emotions/feelings.

● **Paint. Circle the letter e.**

Phonemic Awareness

Learning to Know

Hennie Hen

Ellie Elephant

Objectives: Short /e/ sound.

Mathematical Thinking

Learning to Know

Draw one shape with straight lines and one with curved lines.

Objectives: Sort objects.

- **Trace and fill the elephant and egg with paper balls.**

Ee

Draw a line from left to right to match.

Artistic Expression and Appreciation

Learning to Be

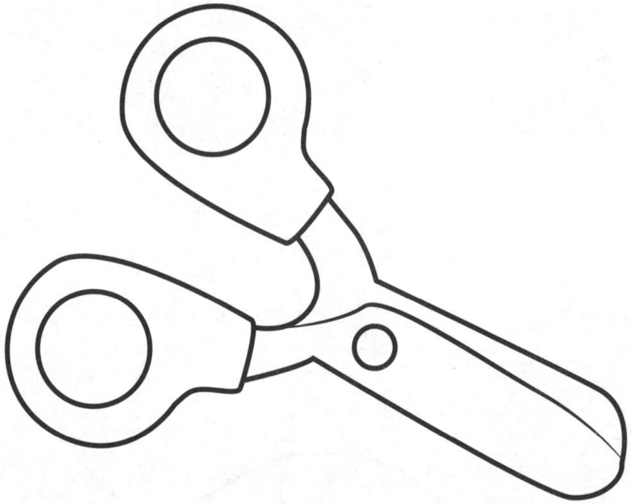

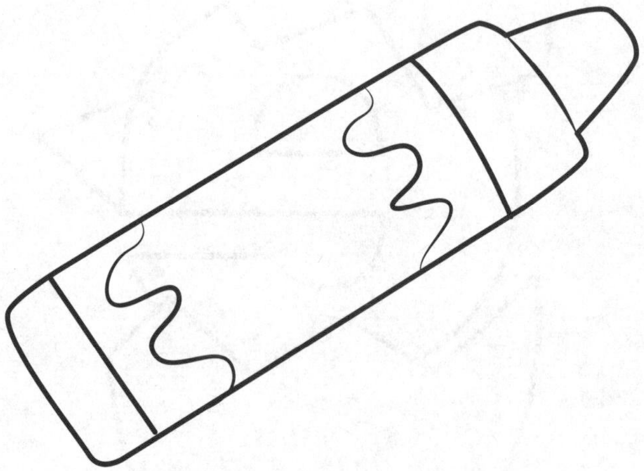

Objectives: Everyday school objects and what they are for.

Lift your arms and leg to make an *E*.

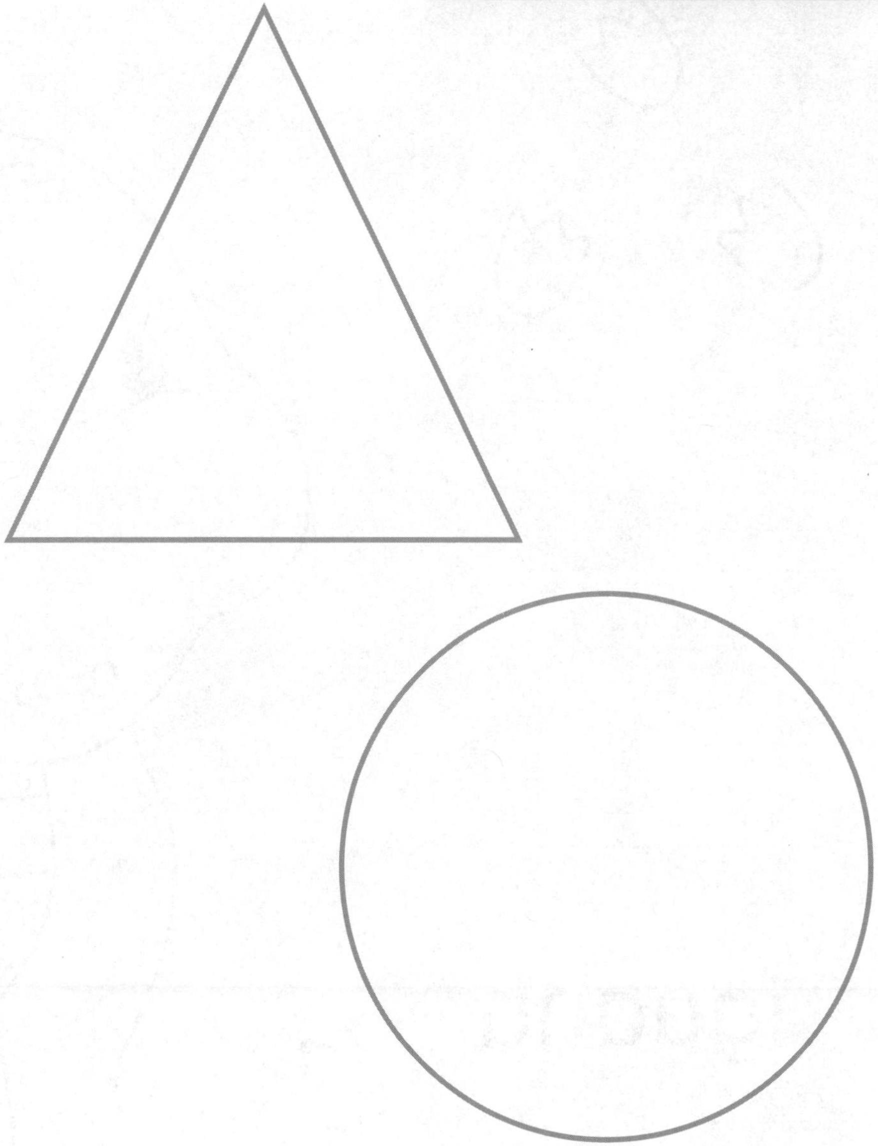

Trace the shapes. Make them with your body.

Objectives: Importance of moving our bodies.

Color the iguana.

i

iguana

Objectives: Short /i/ sound.

Say and match.

Mathematical Thinking

Learning to Know

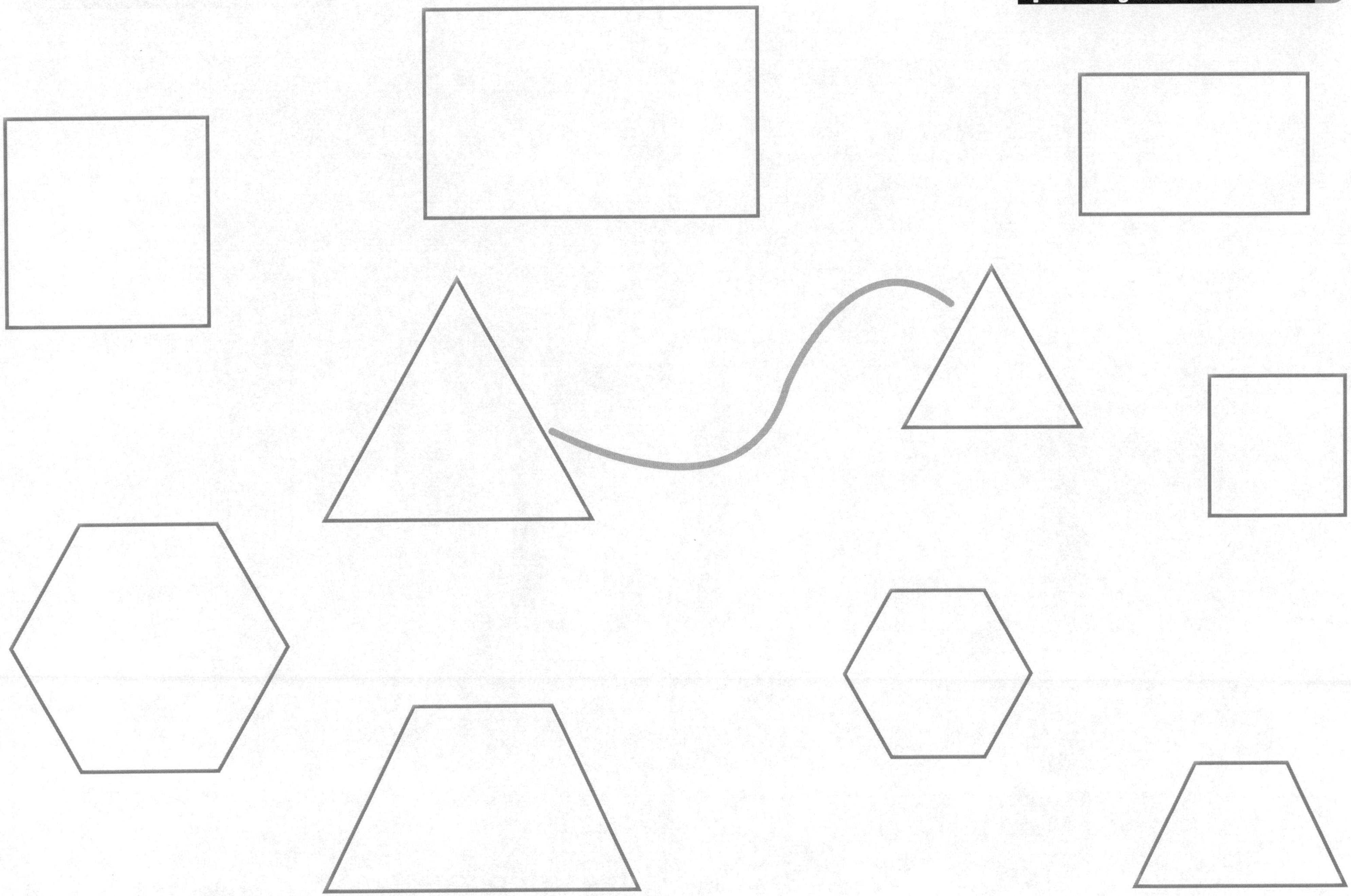

Objectives: Name and match similar shapes.

Trace the letter *i* and the box.

Developmental Writing

Learning to Know

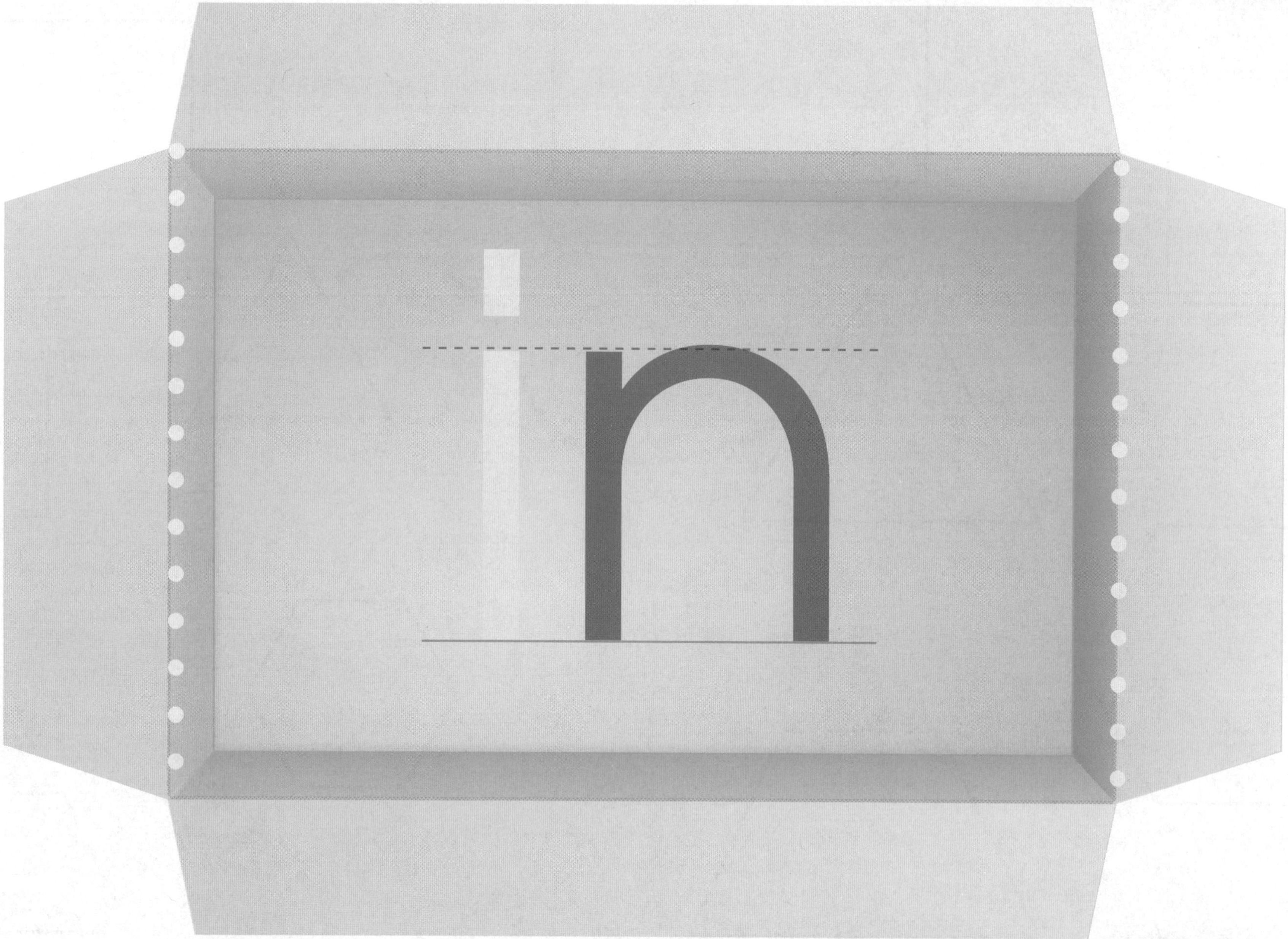

Objectives: Letter *Ii*.

Draw your family.

Artistic Expression and Appreciation

Learning to Be

Objectives: Family members.

Personal, Social, and Emotional Development

Learning to Live Together
Learning to Live with Others

Draw something you like about your family.

Objectives: Family members. Likes.

Trace the letters.

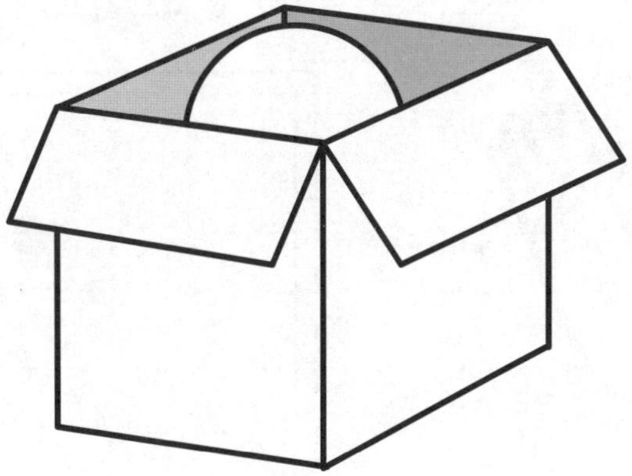

i

in

iguana

igloo

Color where a family can live.

Objectives: Short /i/ sound.

Mathematical Thinking

Learning to Know

Count, color, and match.

3

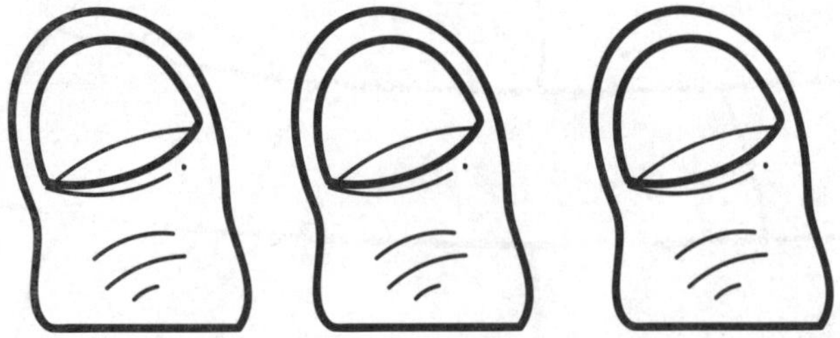

2

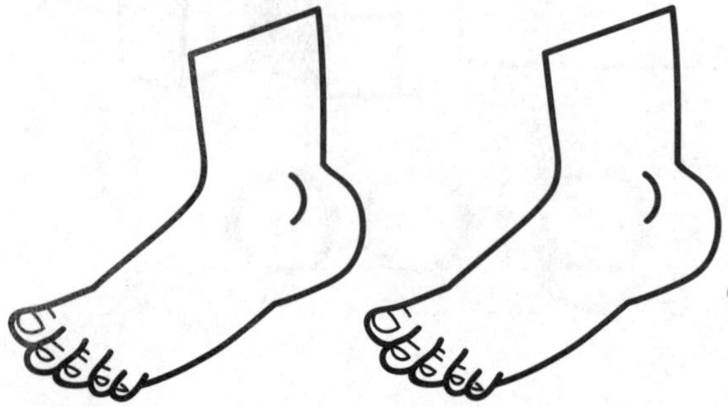

4

Objectives: Match objects and numbers.

Developmental Writing

Learning to Know

Trace the letters. Connect the dots. Color the big square.

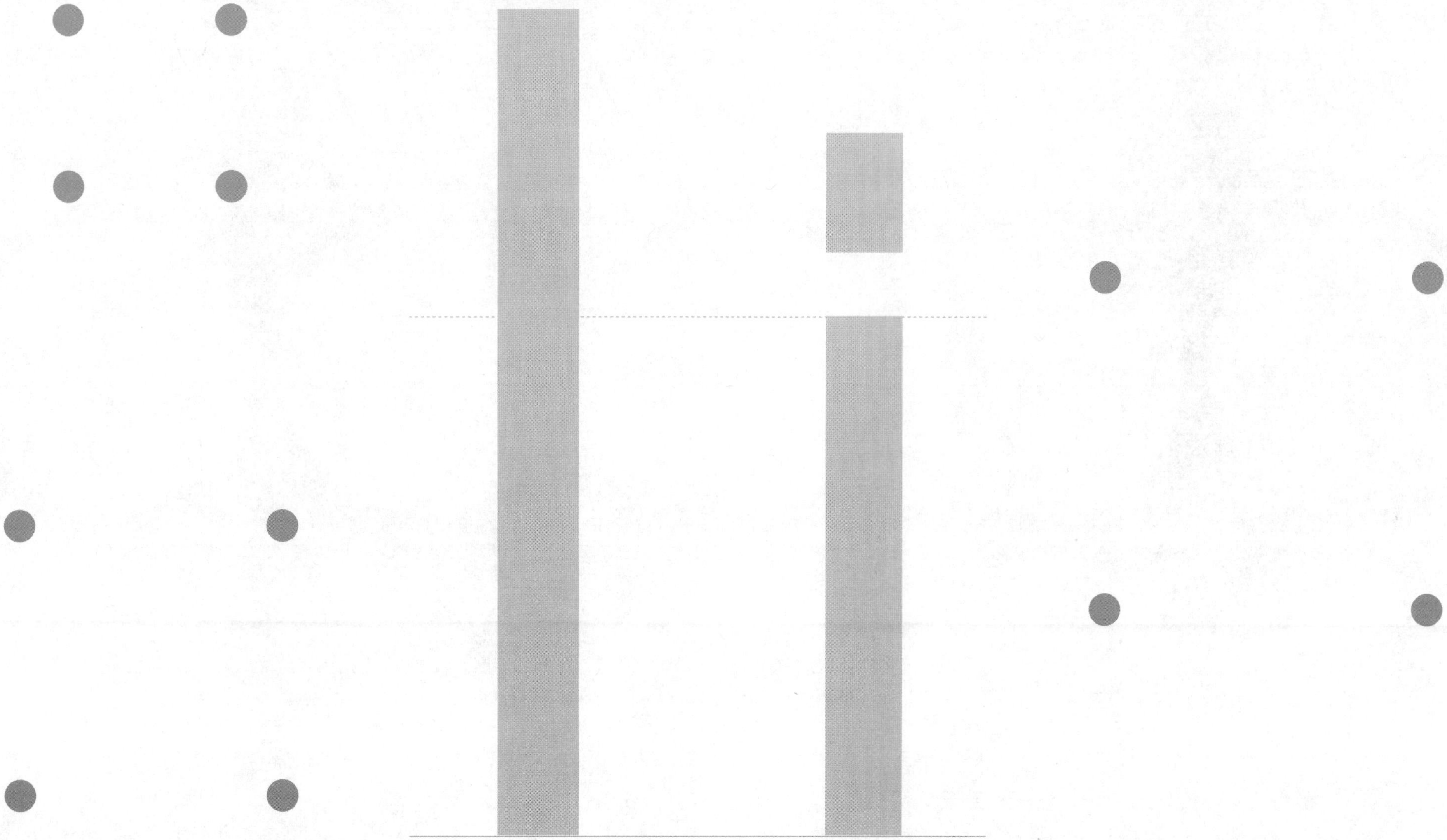

Objectives: Lines. Squares. Letter *Ii.*

Color the different one in each row.

Artistic Expression and Appreciation

Learning to Be

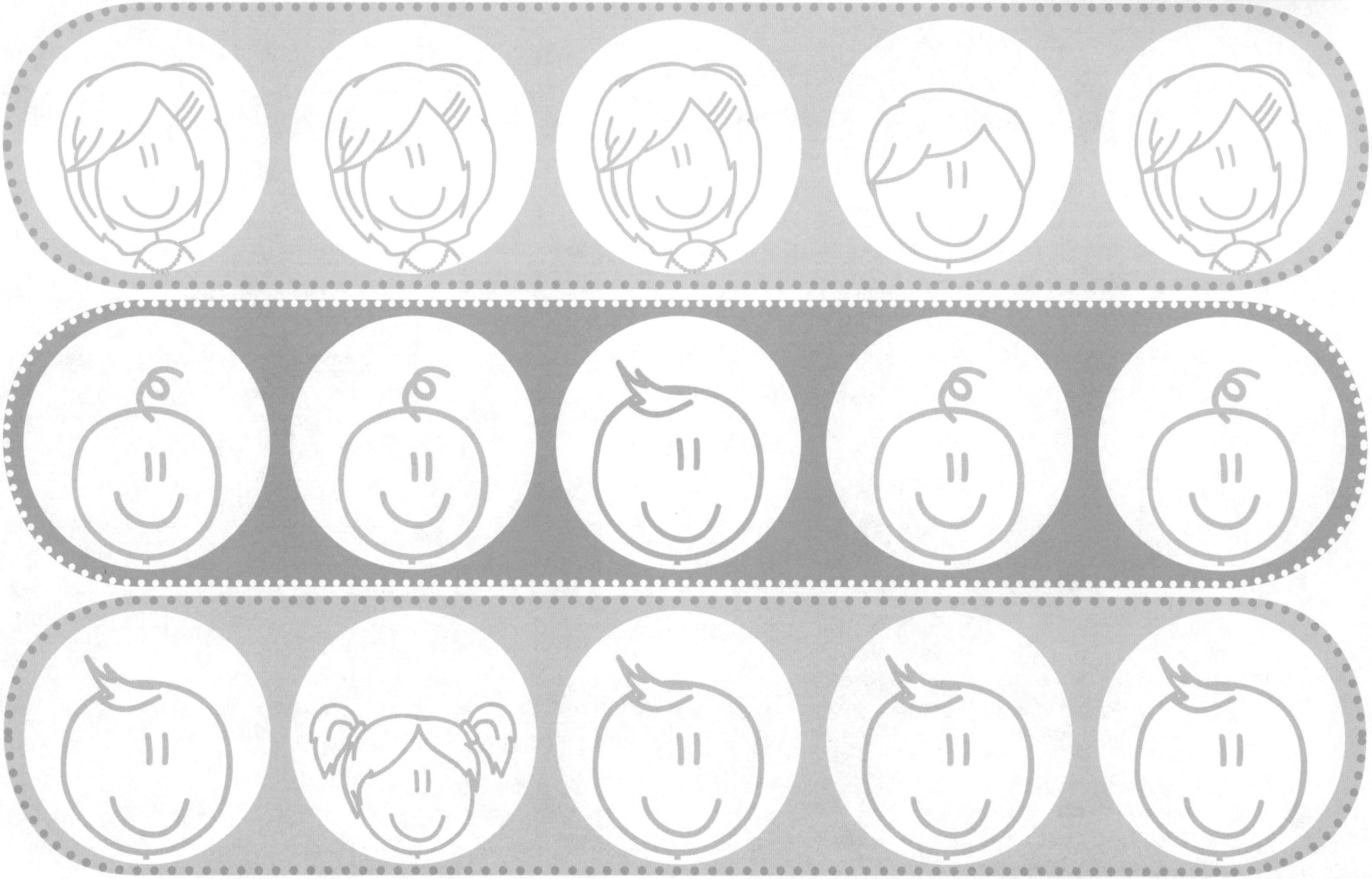

Objectives: Family members.

What do kittens like? Draw the things they like.

Exploration and Knowing of the World

Learning to Do

What can you see? Match the pictures.

Phonemic Awareness

Learning to Know

Finger paint the big pictures.

Objectives: Short /i/ sound.

Draw. The dog is in the house. The cat is out of the house.

Paste pieces of colored paper on the house.

Trace the letters and shapes.

Developmental Writing

Learning to Know

Igloo igloo

Objectives: Circles. Squares. Letter *Ii*.

Draw his family.

Artistic Expression and Appreciation

Learning to Be

Objectives: Family members.

Color the pictures you like.

Personal, Social, and Emotional Development

Learning to Live Together
Learning to Live with Others

Objectives: Likes and dislikes.

What's in the igloo? Trace the letters and color.

Phonemic Awareness

Learning to Know

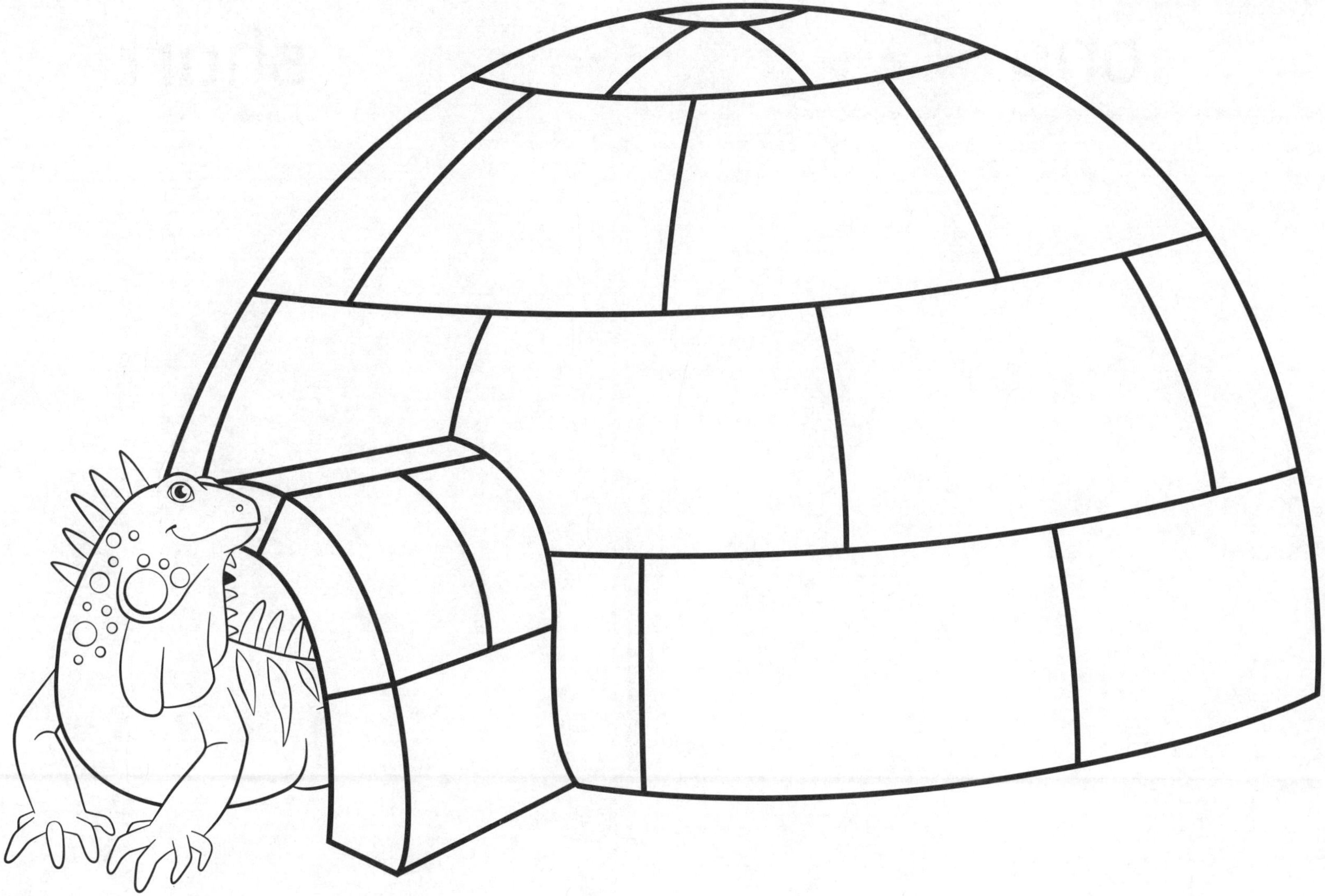

An iguana in the igloo.

Objectives: Short /i/ sound.

Mathematical Thinking

Learning to Know

Cut and paste long and short objects.

long

short

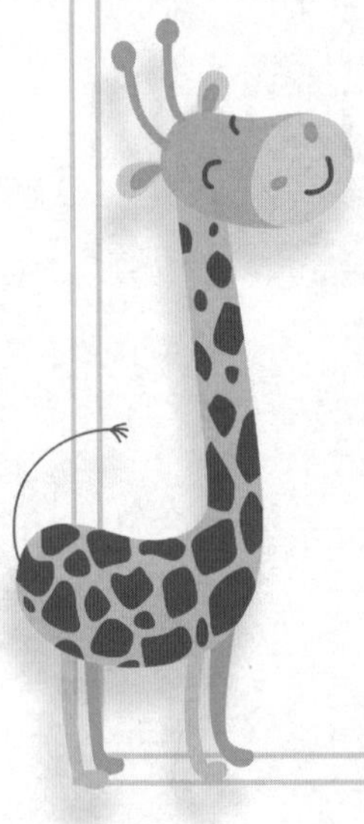

Objectives: Sort objects by length.

Color the letters with dots.

Developmental Writing

Learning to Know

Objectives: Lines. Letter *Ii.*

Finger paint the kids. Draw a pet.

Artistic Expression and Appreciation

Learning to Be

Objectives: Family members.

Trace the letter and color the heart.

Personal, Social, and Emotional Development

Learning to Live Together
Learning to Live with Others

I ♡ my family

Color the members of your family.

Objectives: Different kind of families.

Phonemic Awareness

Learning to Know

Draw a line between each toy and letter. Color the toys.

a

e

i

Objectives: Short /a/, /e/, /i/.

Sort the pictures.

Mathematical Thinking

Learning to Know

Objectives: Sort sets of objects.

Trace the shapes and the letters.

Developmental Writing

Learning to Know

Color two shapes blue and one red.

Objectives: Triangles. Letter *a*.

Artistic Expression and Appreciation

Learning to Be

What can you see? Color the toy you like most.

Use clay to make your favorite toy.

Objectives: Make toys.

Draw your favorite toy.

Physical Development and Health

Learning to Be

Come play with me!

Objectives: Social awareness of oneself and objects.

Color the toys that are in the toy box.

Phonemic Awareness

Learning to Know

Objectives: Short /a/, /e/, /i/.

Mathematical Thinking

Learning to Know

Draw and color the correct number of circles.

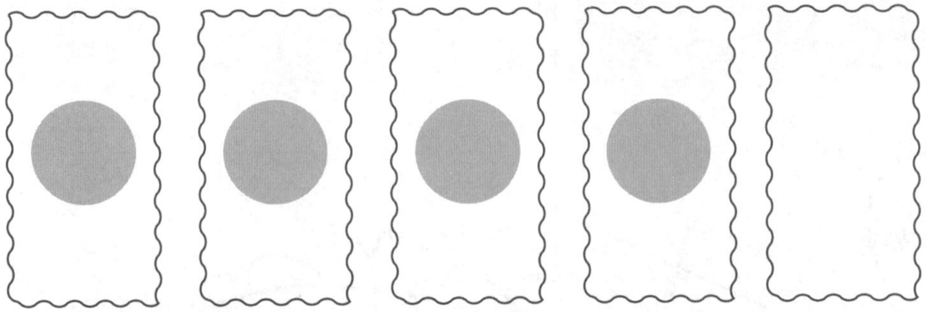

4

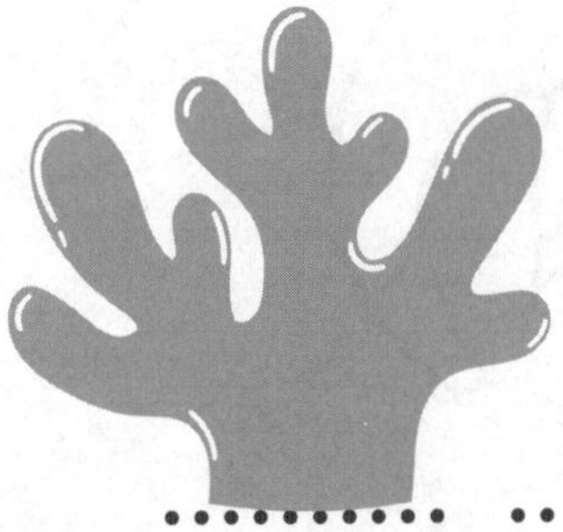

2

5

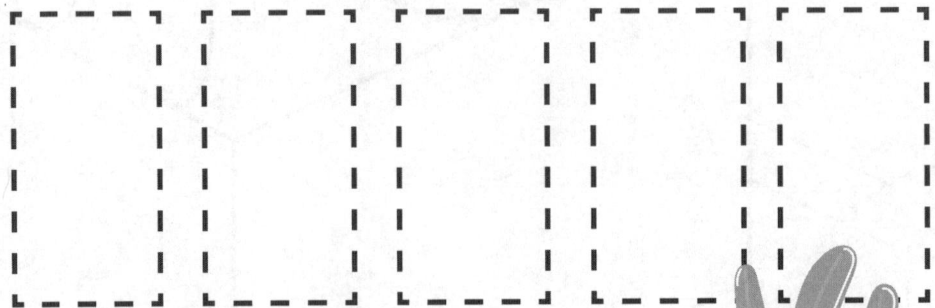

3

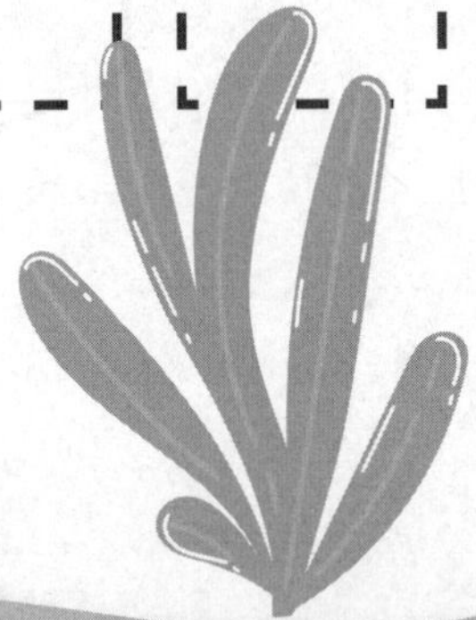

Objectives: Use a five-frame to show amounts to 5.

Trace the letters and toys.

Developmental Writing

Learning to Know

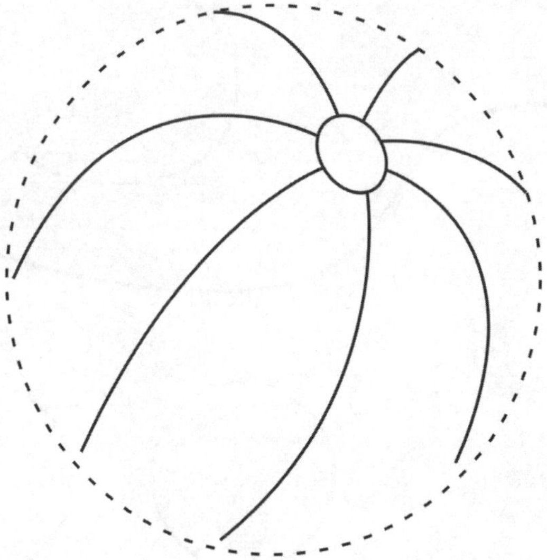

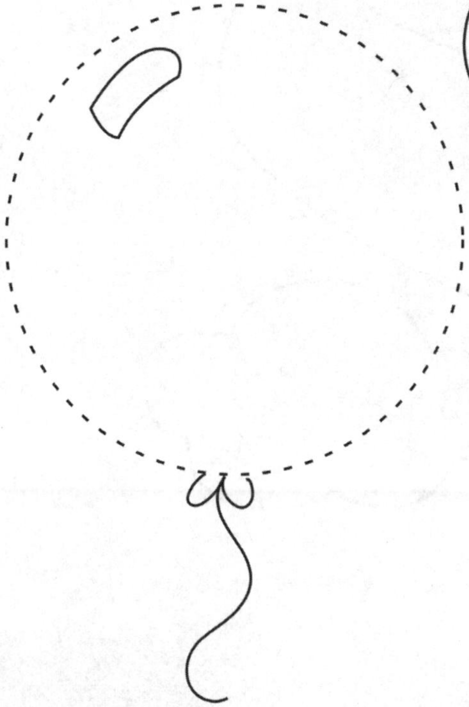

Ae

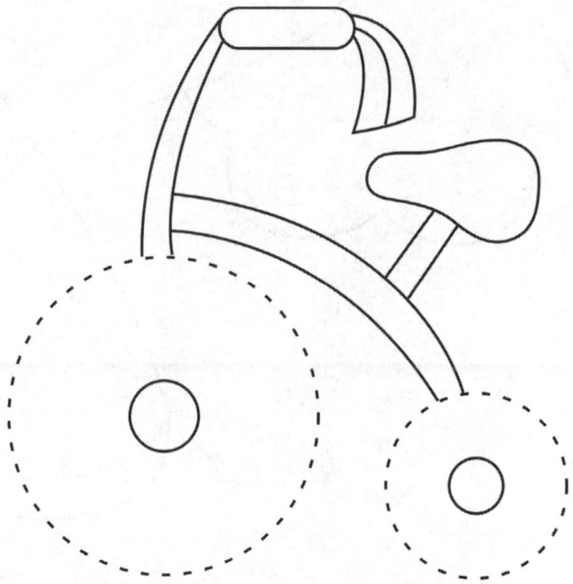

Objectives: Lines. Circles.

Artistic Expression and Appreciation

Learning to Be

Draw the plane.

Fingerpaint the plane and sky.

Objectives: Make toys.

Physical Development and Health

Learning to Be

Color the balls blue, yellow, and red.

Draw what you do with a ball.

Objectives: Social awareness of oneself and objects.

Phonemic Awareness

Learning to Know

Match the pictures to their initial letter. Trace.

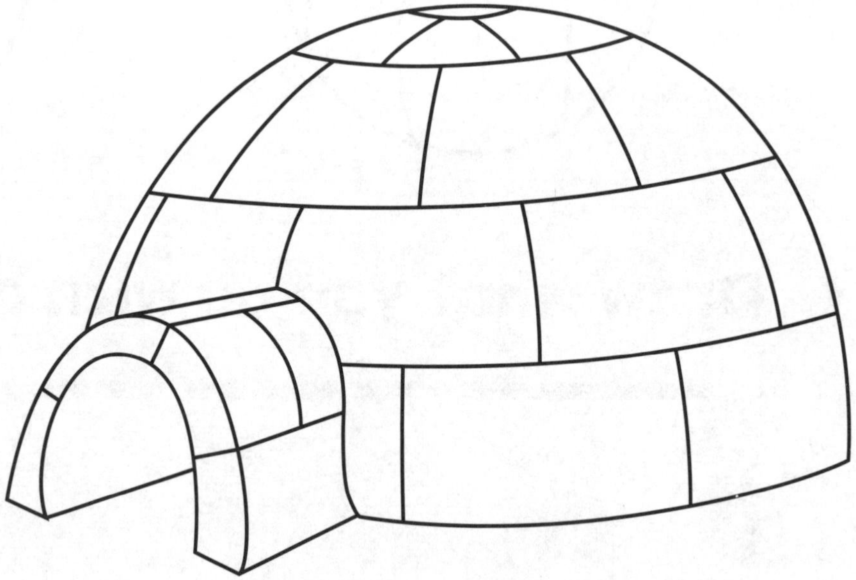

a e i

Objectives: Short /a/, /e/, /i/.

Trace 5 times.

Objectives: Trace numbers 1 and 2.

Complete the letters. Use different colors.

Objectives: Lines *a*, *e*, *i*.

Paste paper on the wheels of the tricycle.

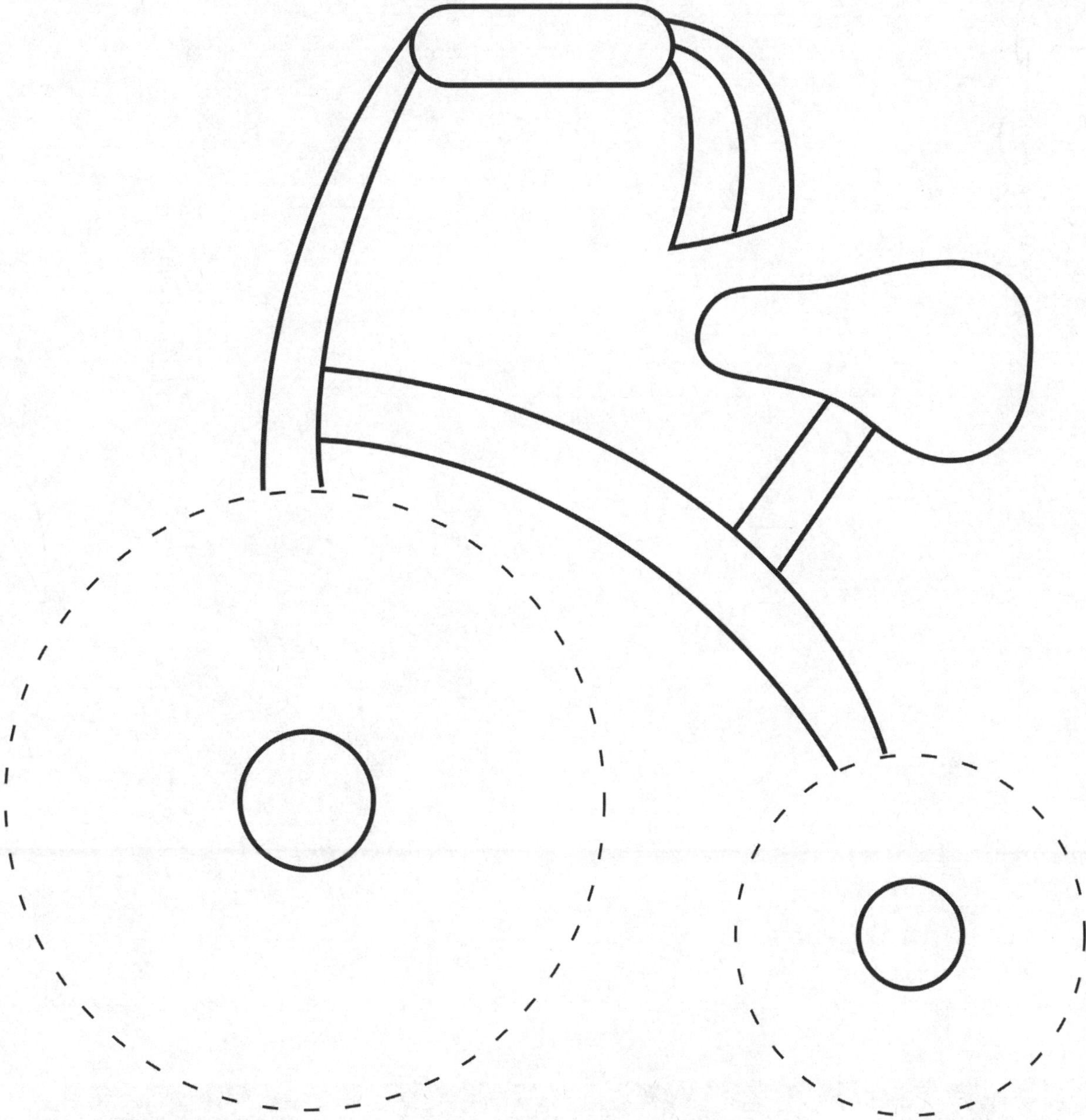

Objectives: Make toys.

Draw a ball. Color it orange.

Physical Development and Health

Learning to Be

Objectives: Interact with others.

Draw pictures of words that begin with *a*, *e* and *i*.

Objectives: Short /a/, /e/, /i/.

Follow the patterns.

Mathematical Thinking

Learning to Know

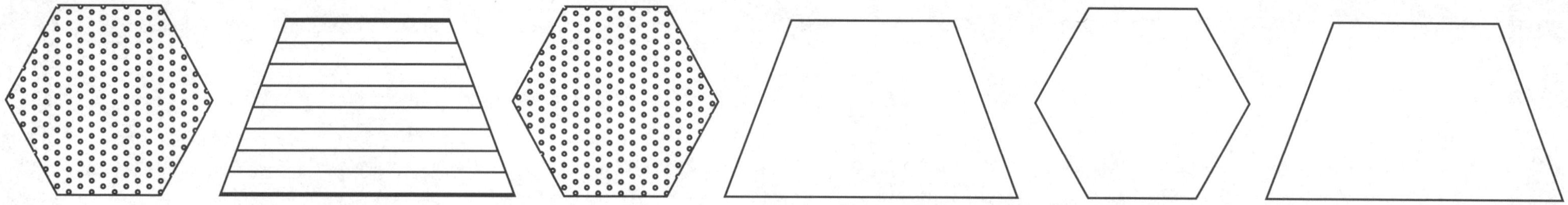

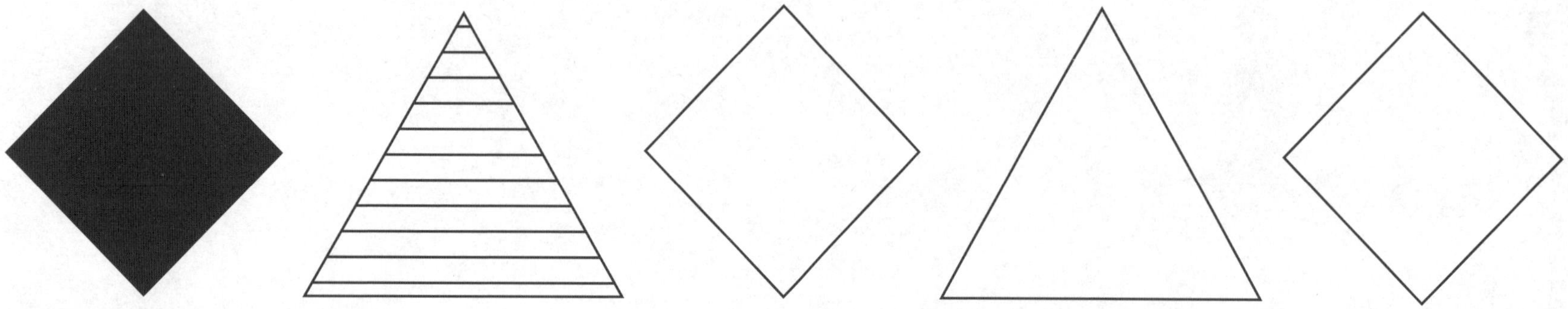

Objectives: Identify and extend simple patterns.

Developmental Writing

Learning to Know

Trace the letters. Use blue, red, and orange.

a a a a a

e e e e e

i

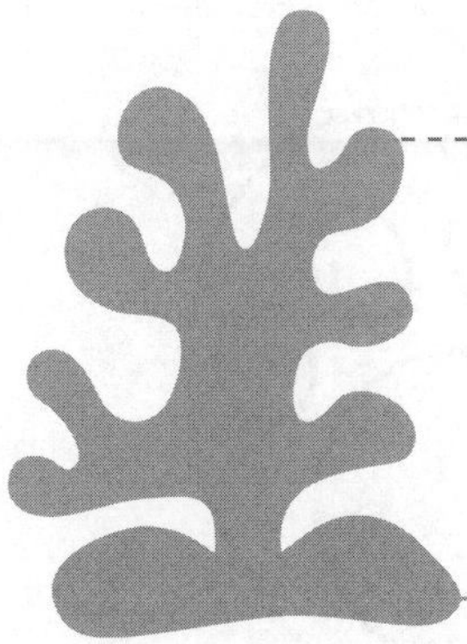

i i i i

Draw the missing parts. Color.

Artistic Expression and Appreciation

Learning to Be

Objectives: Make toys.

Do you put your toys away? Yes or no? Color the picture.

Objectives: Care for one's belongings.

Trace the letters. Paste paper on the iguana.

a a i e i
a
e
i a

i

e

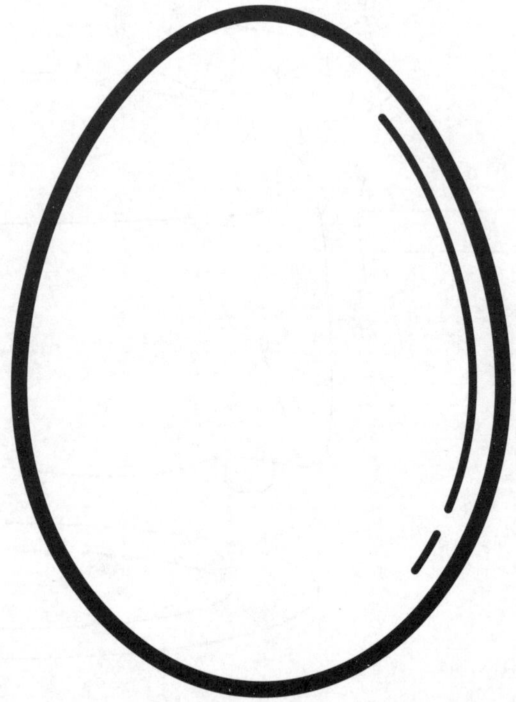

Color the egg.

Objectives: Short /a/, /e/, /i/.

Count, color, and match.

4

3

5

2

Objectives: Match number to objects.

Developmental Writing

Learning to Know

Trace the letters. Trace the shapes in different colors.

Objectives: Lines. Triangles. Squares. Letters *a*, *e*, *i*.

Color the robot. Draw the robot doing your favorite activity.

Artistic Expression and Appreciation

Learning to Be

Objectives: Make toys.

Physical Development and Health

Learning to Be

Match the **BIG** toys to the small toys.

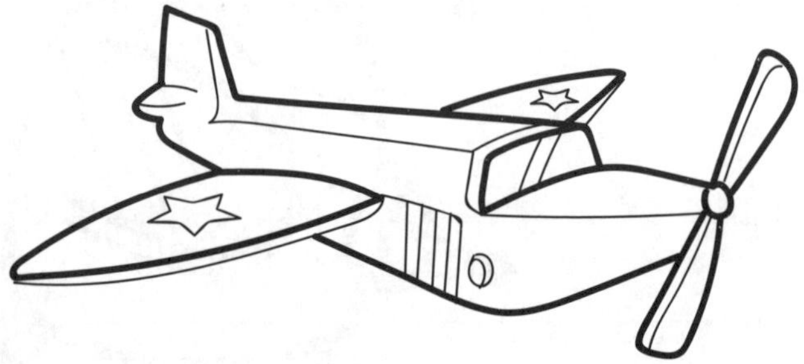

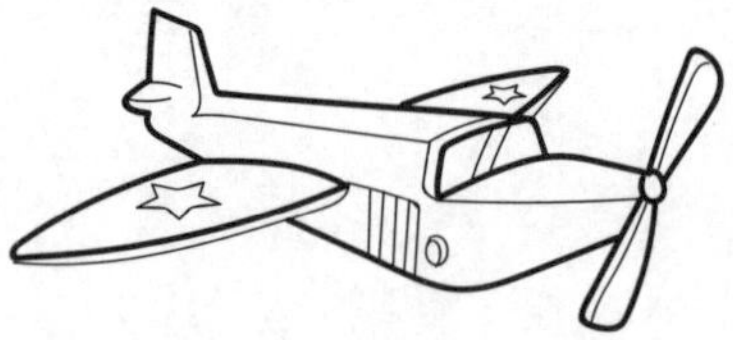

Finger paint the toys you want to share.

Objectives: Identify characteristics.

Color the big toy blue and the small toys yellow. Match the name to the toy.

Phonemic Awareness
Learning to Know

Objectives: Short /a/, /e/, /i/.

Color short. Cross out tall.

Mathematical Thinking

Learning to Know

Objectives: Identify tall and short.

Developmental Writing

Learning to Know

Trace and color the shapes. Draw a small shape inside each shape.

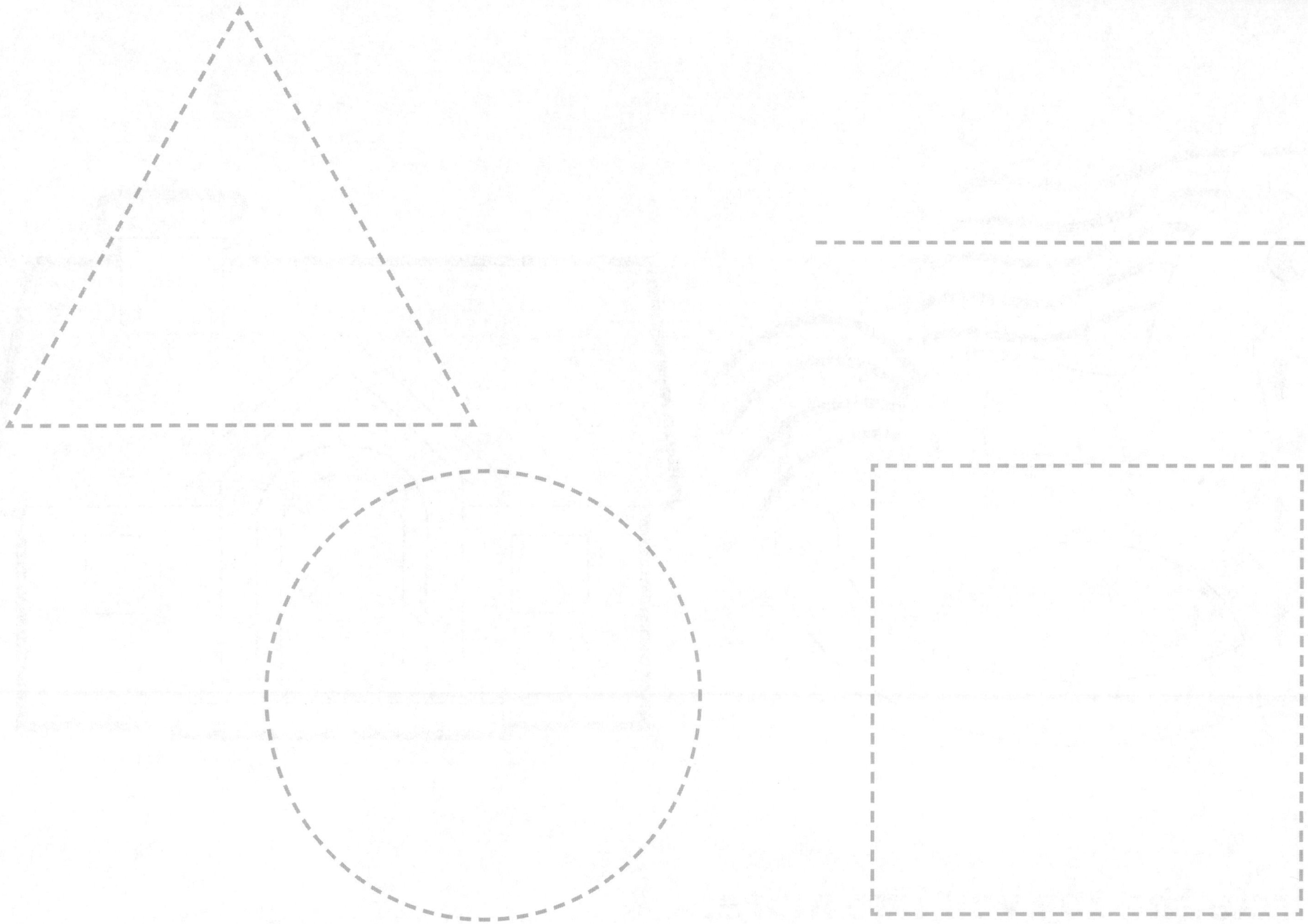

Objectives: Lines. Squares. Circles. Triangles.

Artistic Expression and Appreciation

Learning to Be

- **Color the toys. Paste string on the lines.**

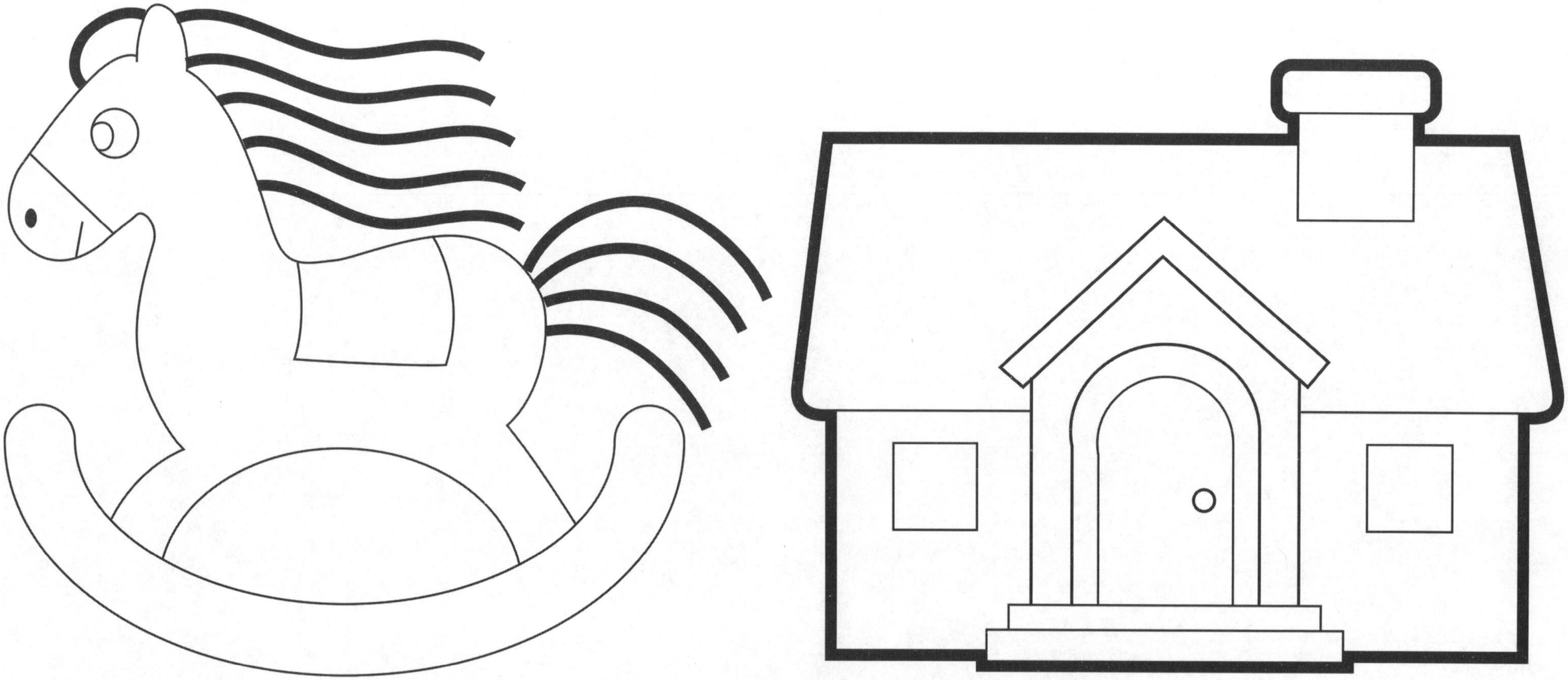

- **Circle the toy you like more.**

Objectives: Make toys.

Number the pictures and tell the story.

Objectives: Care for one's belongings.

Draw and finger paint a house for the octopus. Trace.

Phonemic Awareness

Learning to Know

Objectives: Short /o/ sound.

Mathematical Thinking

Learning to Know

Extend the pattern.

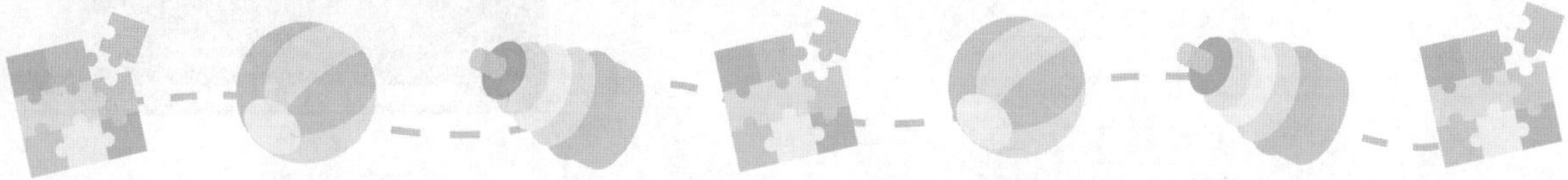

Objectives: Recognize and extend a simple pattern.

● **Trace the shapes. Find the *o*s. Color.**

Developmental Writing

Learning to Know

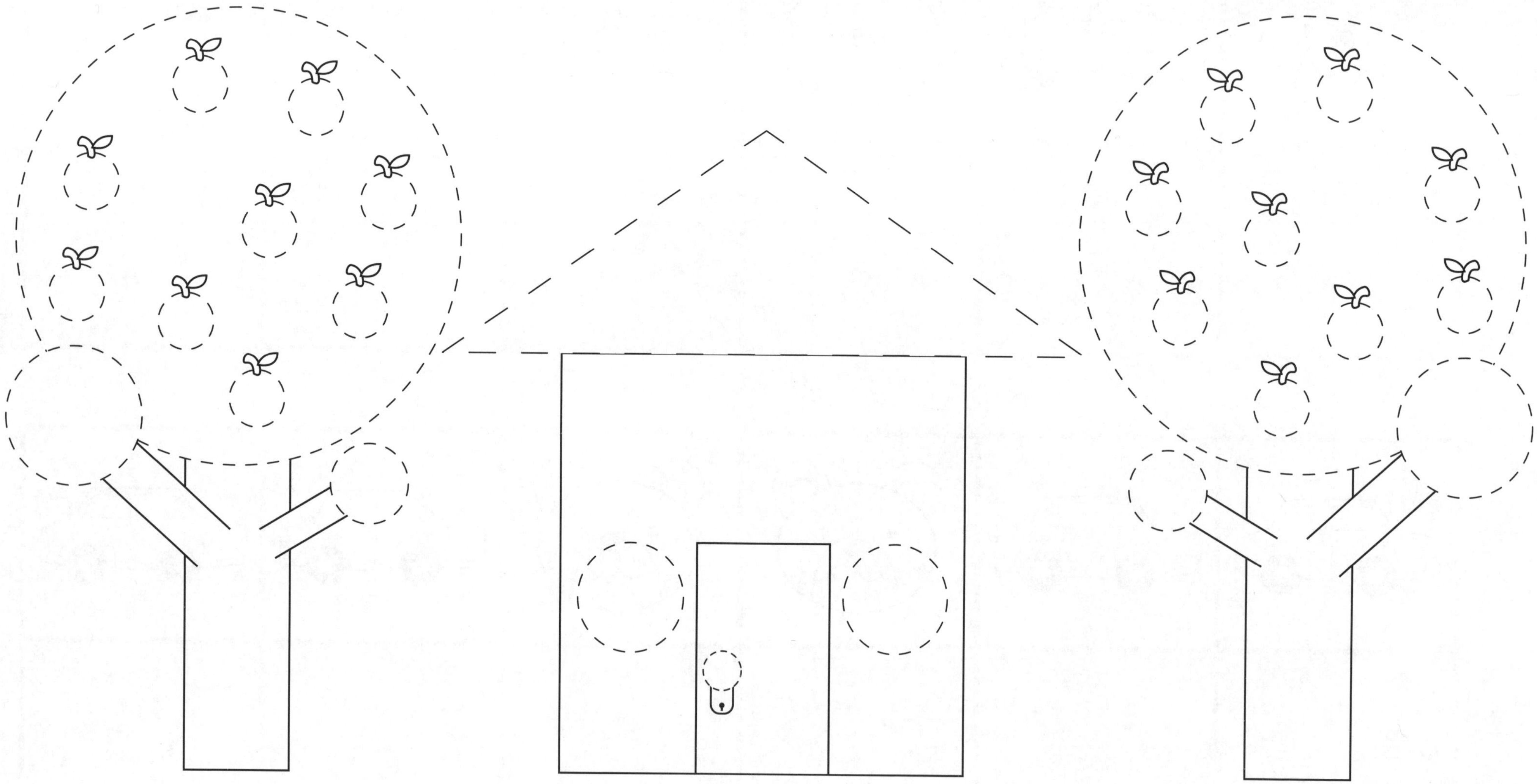

Objectives: Triangles. Lines. Letter *o*.

Trace and color the bed.

Draw your favorite toy on the bed.

Objectives: Rooms in the house.

Color the light that is *on* yellow.

Physical Development and Health

Learning to Be

on

off

Objectives: Chores at home.

Read the sentence and color.

Phonemic Awareness
Learning to Know

The ostrich is orange.

Mathematical Thinking

Learning to Know

Color the big object red and the little object orange.

Objectives: Identify big and little.

Trace the house, tree, and oranges.

Developmental Writing

Learning to Know

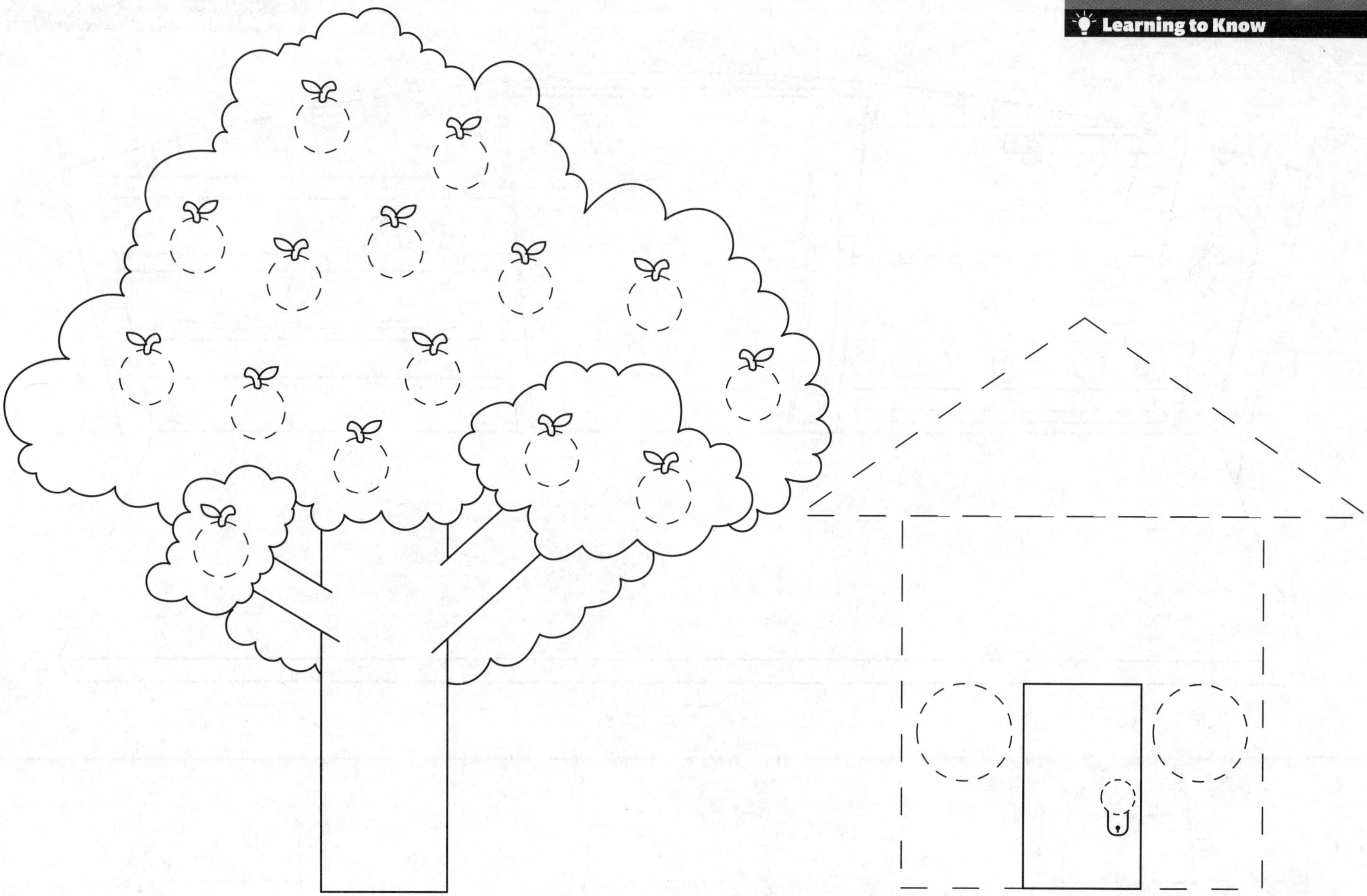

Color the oranges orange. Color the triangle red.

Objectives: Triangles. Lines. Letter o.

Trace the chairs. Draw your favorite food on the table.

Artistic Expression and Appreciation

Learning to Be

Objectives: Room in a house.

Paste yarn on the broom.

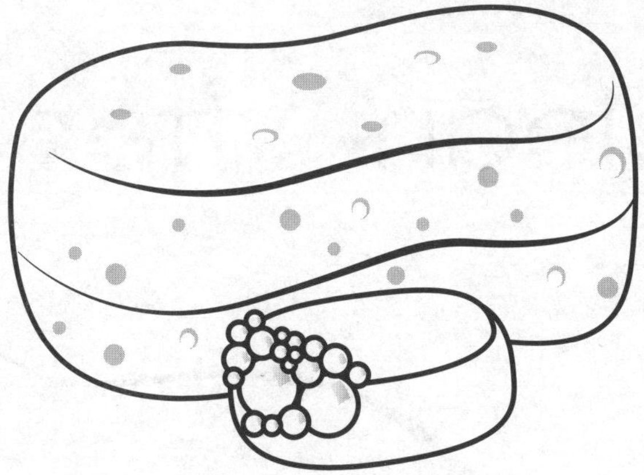

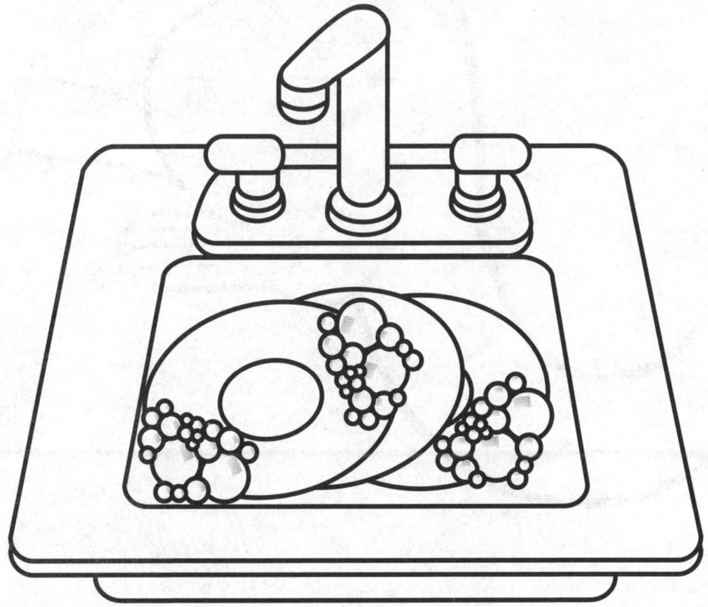

Color what you like to do at home.

Color one otter clean and one dirty. Trace the *o*.

Clean Otter

Dirty Otter

Objectives: Short /o/ sound.

Draw what you do at night.

Mathematical Thinking

Learning to Know

First...

Then...

Objectives: Sequence simple events.

Trace the letters.

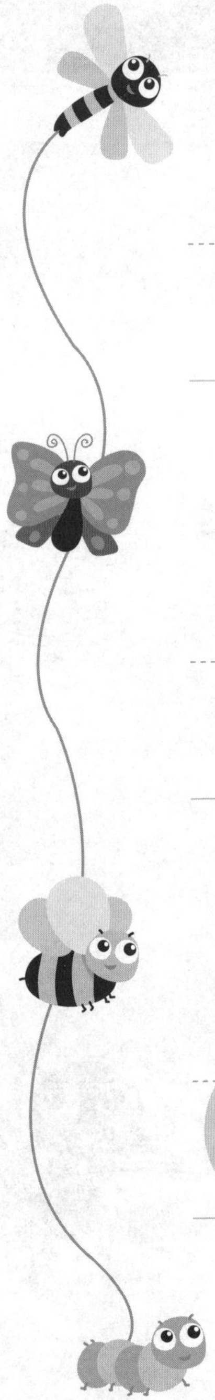

o o o o o o o o o

o o o o o o o o o

O o O o O o O o

Objectives: Letter *o*.

Circle the igloo. Color the houses.

Artistic Expression and Appreciation

Learning to Be

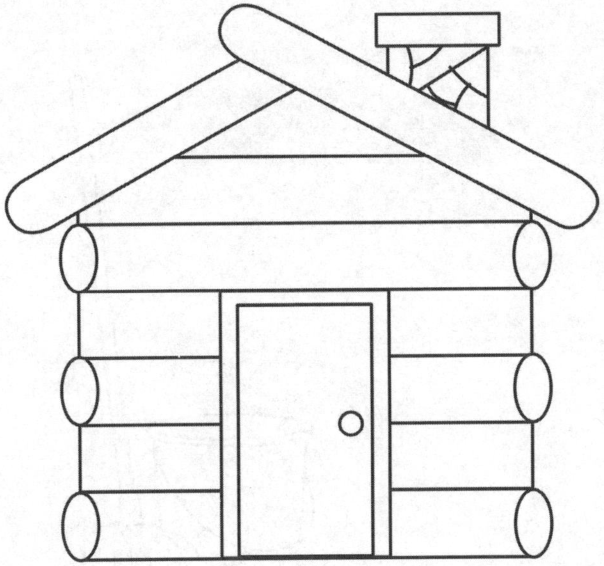

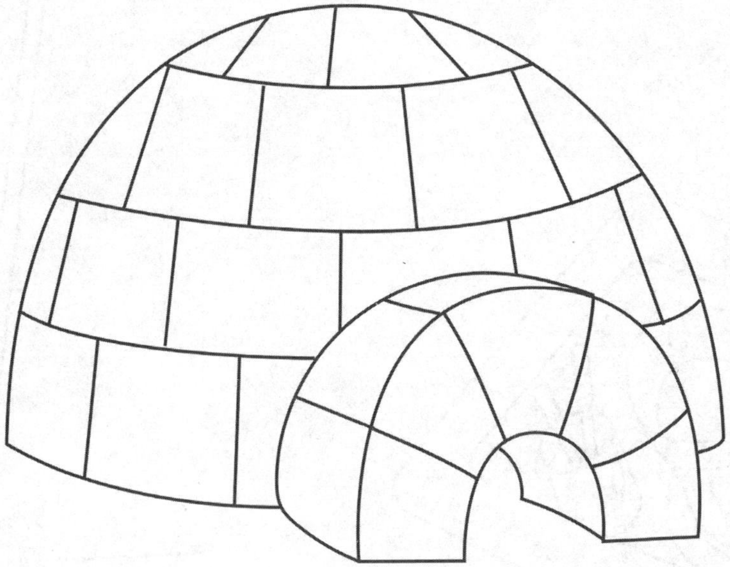

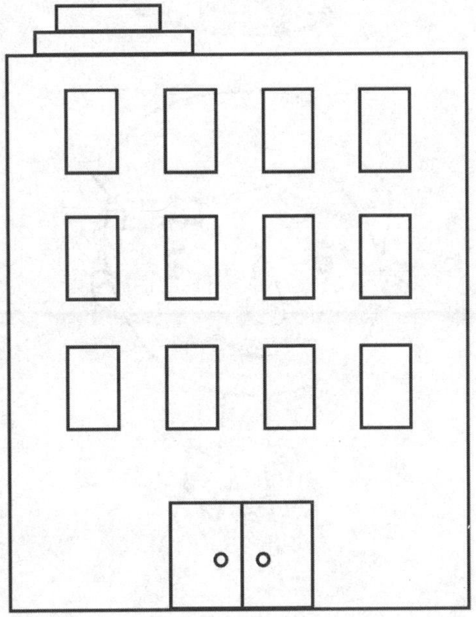

Objectives: Types of houses.

Physical Development and Health

Learning to Be

Circle the child if you can do it. Circle the mom or dad if you can't do it.

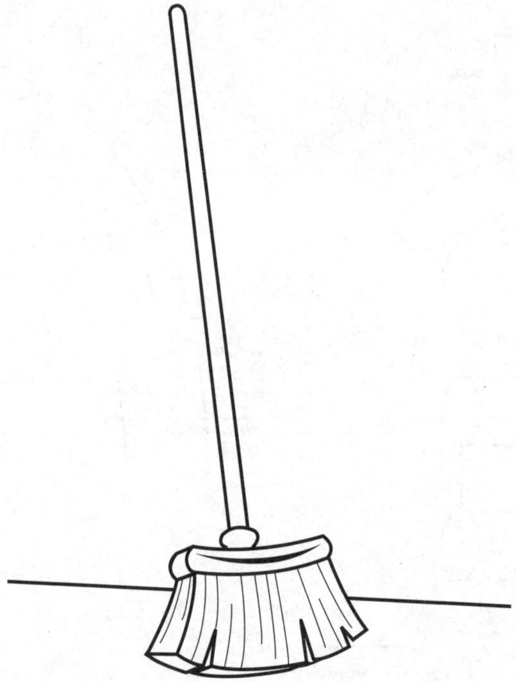

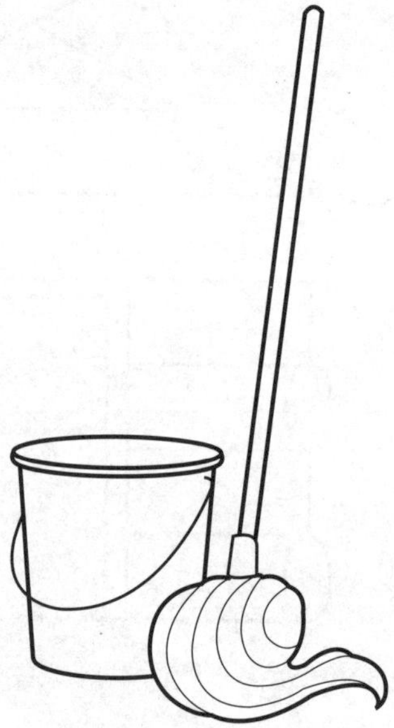

Objectives: Chores they can/can't do at home.

Circle the food the ostrich eats.
Trace the letter.

ostrich

o

Objectives: Short /o/ sound.

Trace the numbers. Draw and count.

Mathematical Thinking

Learning to Know

6

7

Objectives: Match numbers with objects to 7.

What can you see? Where can you find them?

orange

olive

otter

Trace the letters.

The words start with letter ____ .

Objectives: Letter *o*.

Artistic Expression and Appreciation

Learning to Be

Draw what you like to clean at home.

Finger paint your picture.

Objectives: Chores.

Match the things and actions.

Personal, Social, and Emotional Development

Learning to Live Together
Learning to Live with Others

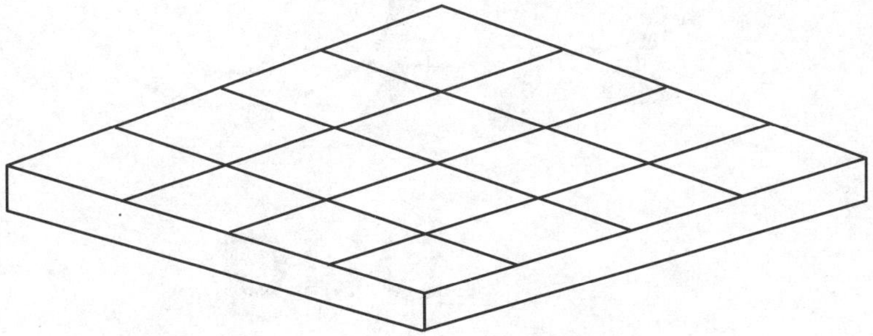

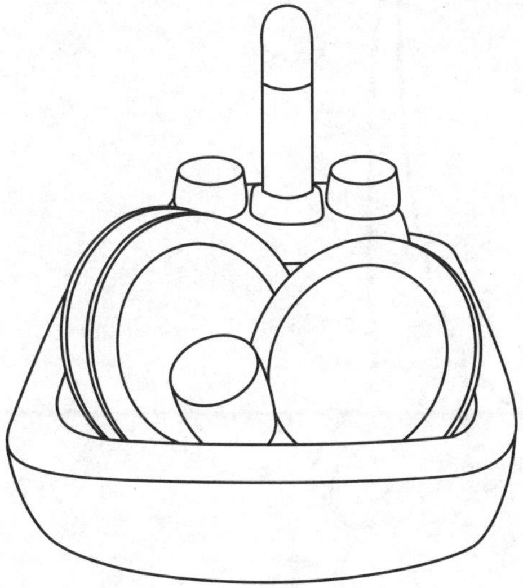

Color the things you like doing.

Finger paint the pet.

Phonemic Awareness

Learning to Know

pup

u

bug

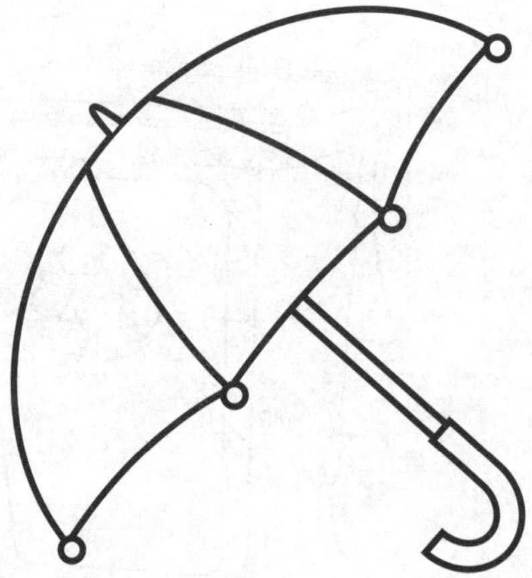

umbrella

Objectives: Short /u/ sound.

Complete the pattern.

Mathematical Thinking

Learning to Know

Objectives: Extend patterns.

Developmental Writing

Learning to Know

- Trace the letters with finger paint.

u u u u

- Trace the letters with crayons.

u u u u

- Paste string on the letters.

u u u u

Objectives: Letter *u*.

Color the pets that are the same.

Objectives: Pets.

Match the people and their pets.

Color the pet that lives in the water.

Objectives: Having a pet.

Draw raindrops. What do you do when it rains?

umbrella

up

mud

Objectives: Short /u/ sound.

Trace the numbers. Draw and count.

Mathematical Thinking

Learning to Know

5

8

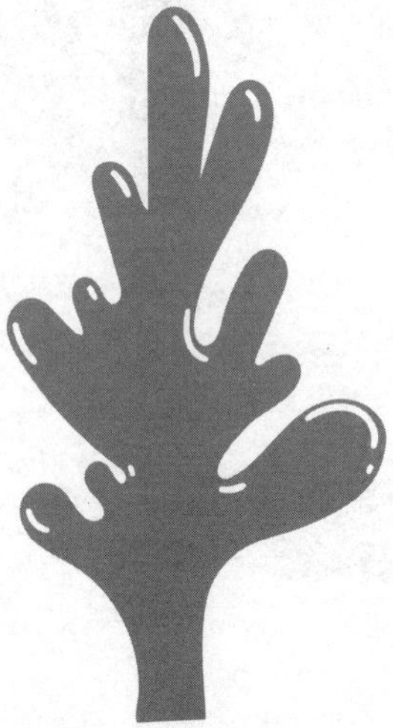

Objectives: Match numbers with objects to 8.

Developmental Writing

Learning to Know

- **Trace the letters.**

u u u

- **Draw a rectangle around the three big letters.**

Artistic Expression and Appreciation

Learning to Be

Color the front and back of each animal. Each animal is a different color.

Objectives: Pets.

Where does each animal live? Match.

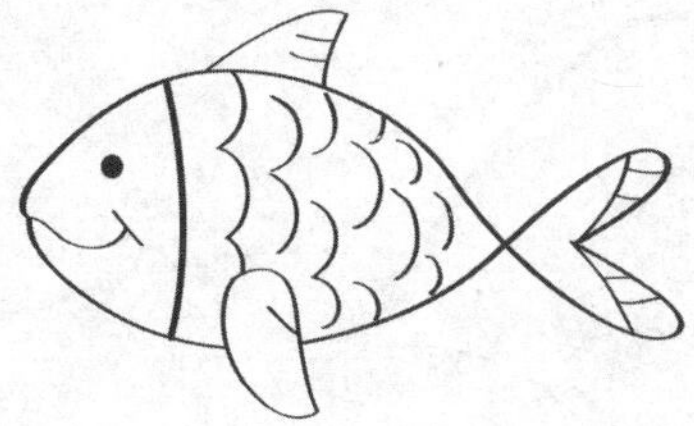

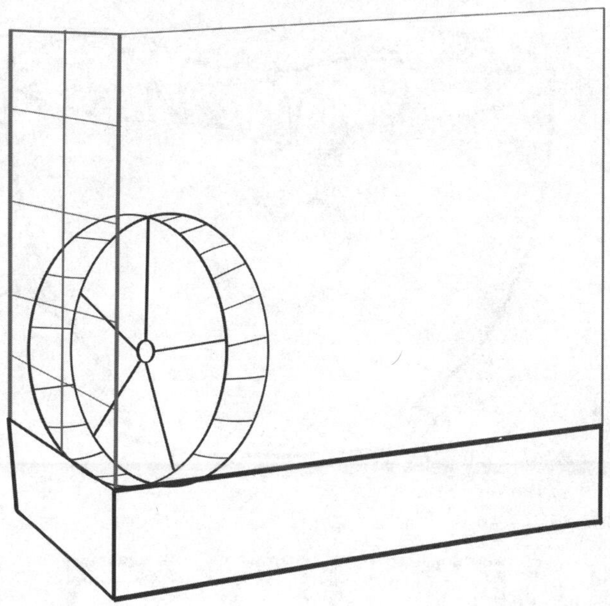

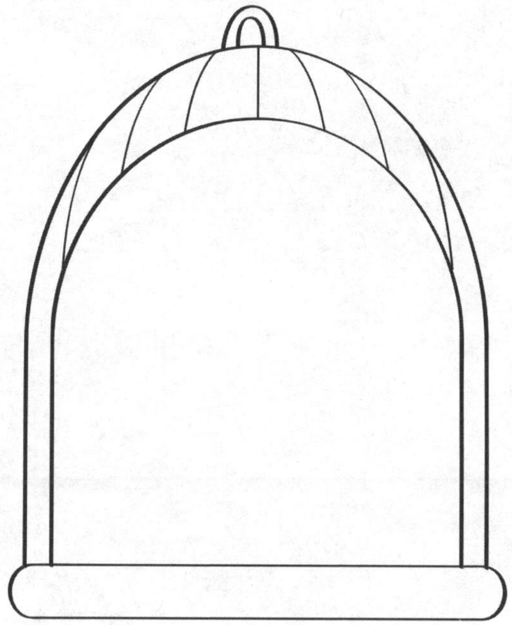

Draw something inside each house.

Objectives: Pet responsibilities.

Phonemic Awareness
Learning to Know

- **Color the pup and the cup.**

A pup in a cup!

- **Trace the *u*'s.**

Objectives: Short *u* sound.

Trace the numbers. Count.

Mathematical Thinking

Learning to Know

Objectives: Write numbers 5, 6, and 7.

Trace the letters.

Developmental Writing

Learning to Know

Uu Uu Uu

Color the turtle.

turtle

turtle

turtle

Objectives: Rectangle. Letter *u*.

Whose food is it? Draw the pets.

Personal, Social, and Emotional Development

Learning to Live Together
Learning to Live with Others

Objectives: Food for pets.

Circle who needs help. Color the ball.

Personal, Social, and Emotional Development

Learning to Live Together
Learning to Live with Others

Objectives: Recognize when someone needs help.

Circle the *u*'s. Color the animals.

Phonemic Awareness

Learning to Know

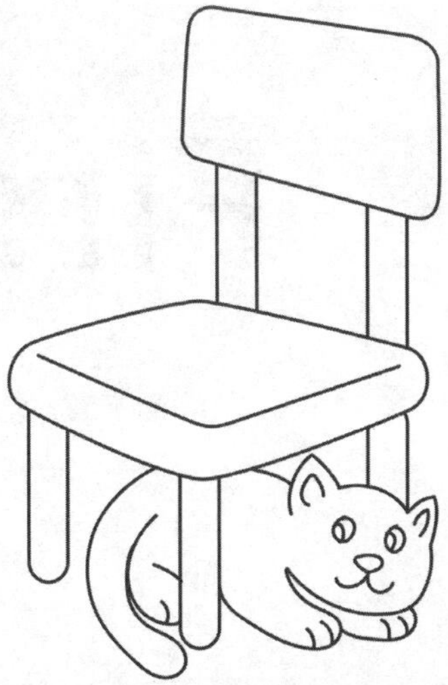

under

duck

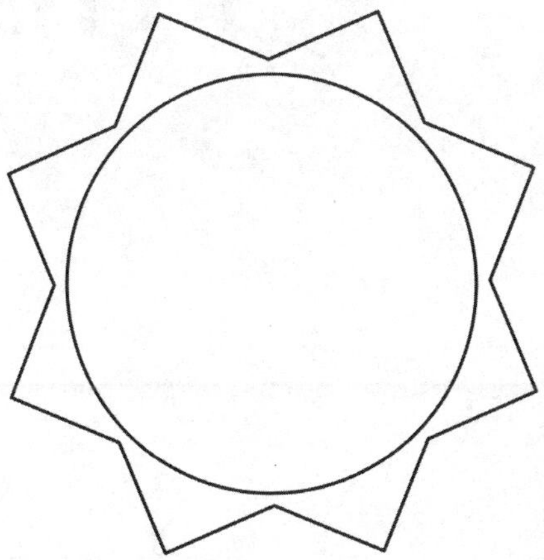

sun

truck

Objectives: Short /u/ sound.

Match the pictures to the words. Color the story.

First...

Then...

Next...

Objectives: Sequence simple events.

Trace the letters and the rectangle.

Uu

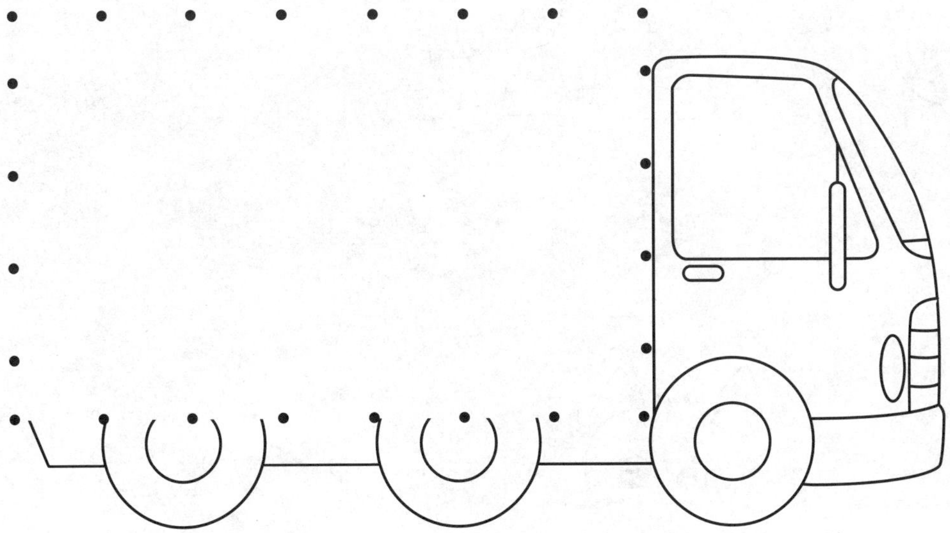

truck

up

Paste paper on the rectangle.

Objectives: Rectangle. Letter *u*.

Match the mothers and babies.

Artistic Expression and Appreciation

Learning to Be

Color the ones you like.

Objectives: Mother animals and babies.

Color the things a dog needs.

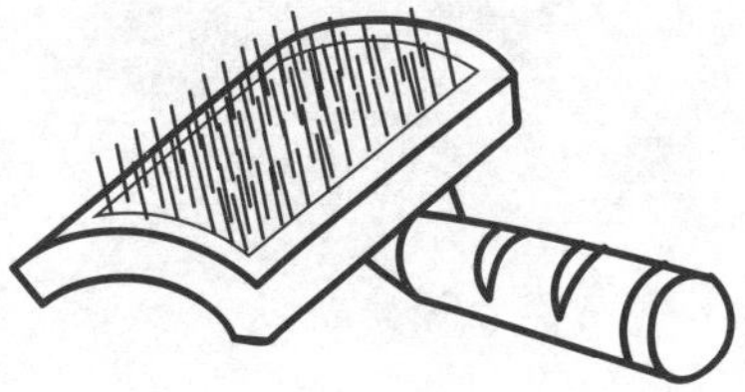
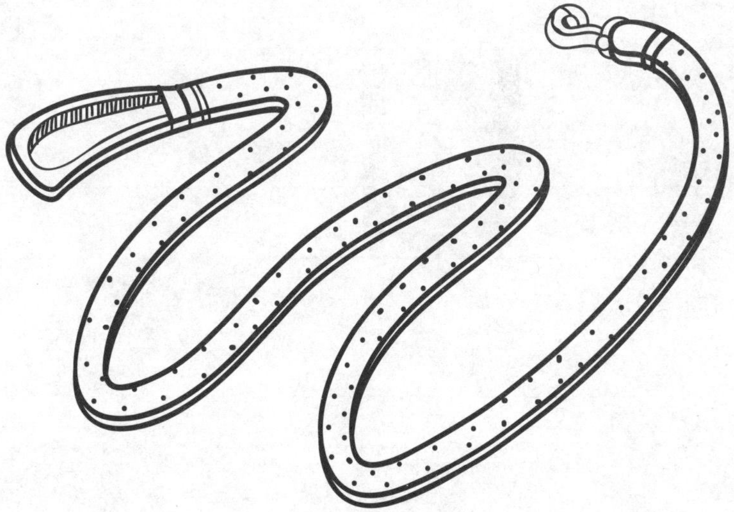
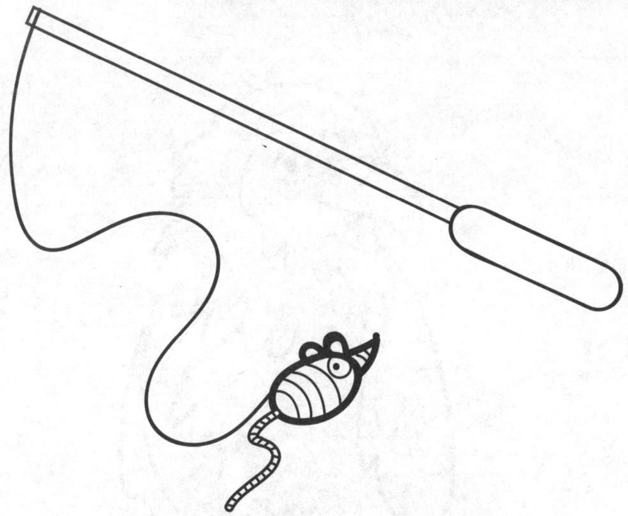

Where is the cat? Circle it.

Phonemic Awareness

Learning to Know

budgie

rug

Objectives: Objectives: Short /*u*/ sound.

Mathematical Thinking

Learning to Know

Sort the objects.

Color the shape that is different.

Developmental Writing

Learning to Know

Complete the words and the rug.

u u

rug rug

Draw lines with different colors in the rug.

Objectives: Lines. Rectangle. Letter *u*.

What is missing? Complete the drawings.

Artistic Expression and Appreciation

Learning to Be

Objectives: Pet activities.

Circle who needs help. Draw how the story ends.

Personal, Social, and Emotional Development

Learning to Live Together
Learning to Live with Others

Objectives: Helping others.

Color the sun. Trace the *u*.

sun

Draw what you like to do in the sun.

Objectives: Short /u/ sound.

Mathematical Thinking

Learning to Know

How long are the carrots? Color and count the squares. Write the numbers.

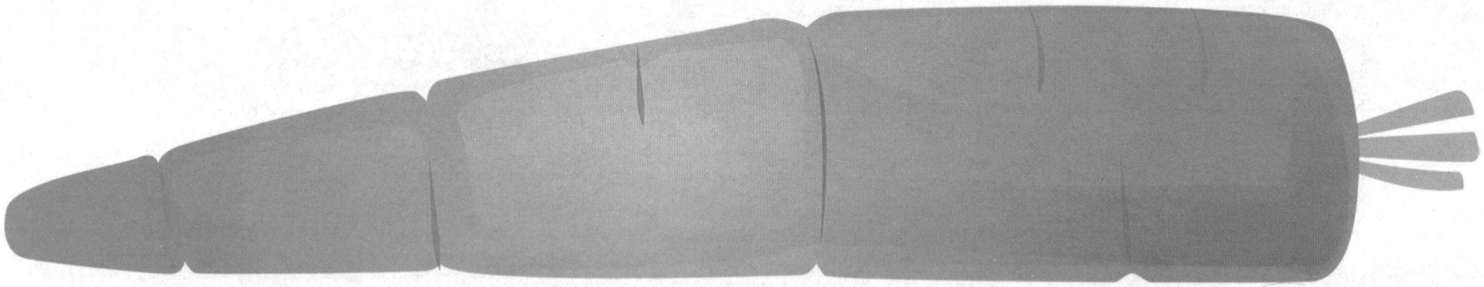

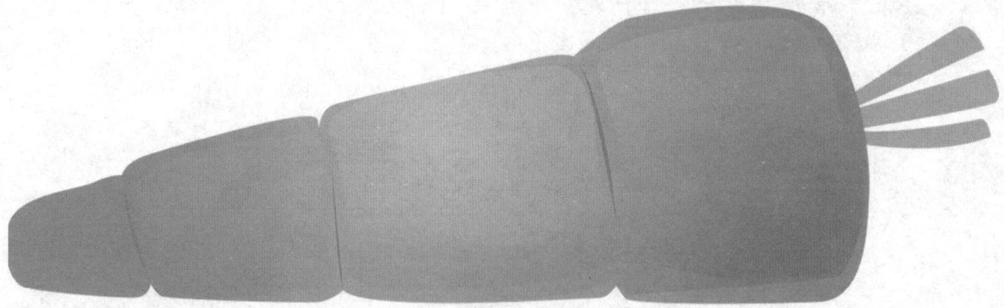

Objectives: Measure using squares.

Developmental Writing

Learning to Know

Paste paper balls on the letters.

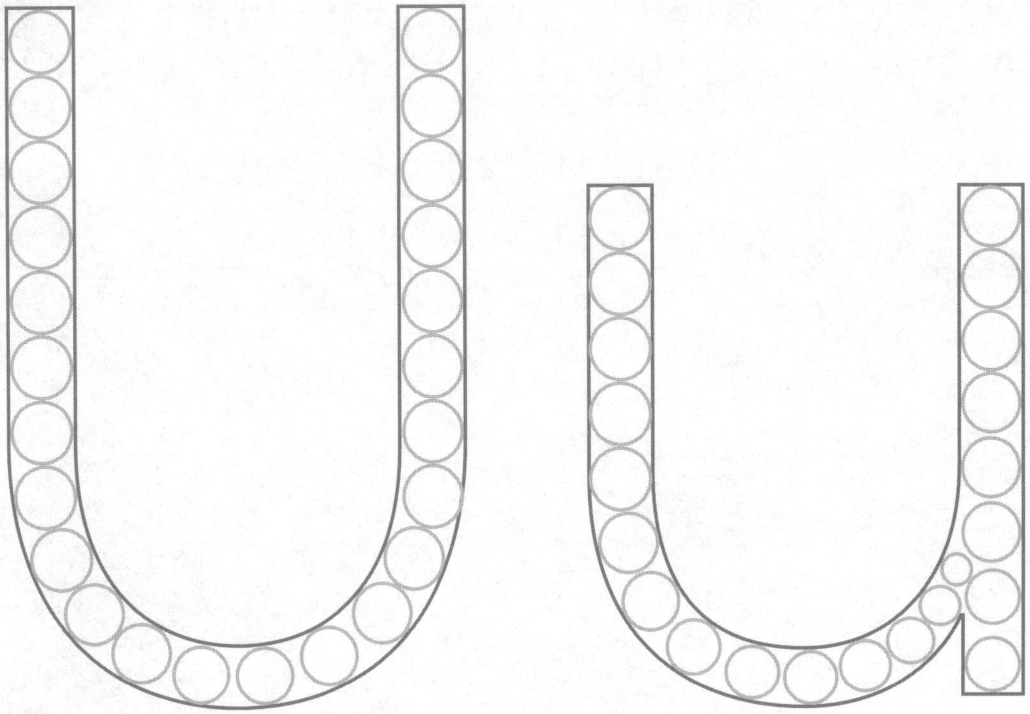

Use crayons to trace the letters.

U u U u U u

Objectives: Letter *u*.

Artistic Expression and Appreciation

Learning to Be

Draw what a pet needs.

I love my pet!

Objectives: Pets needs.

Color the animals you can play with.

Objectives: Pets they can play with.

Phonemic Awareness

Learning to Know

Match the letters and the pictures. Color the food.

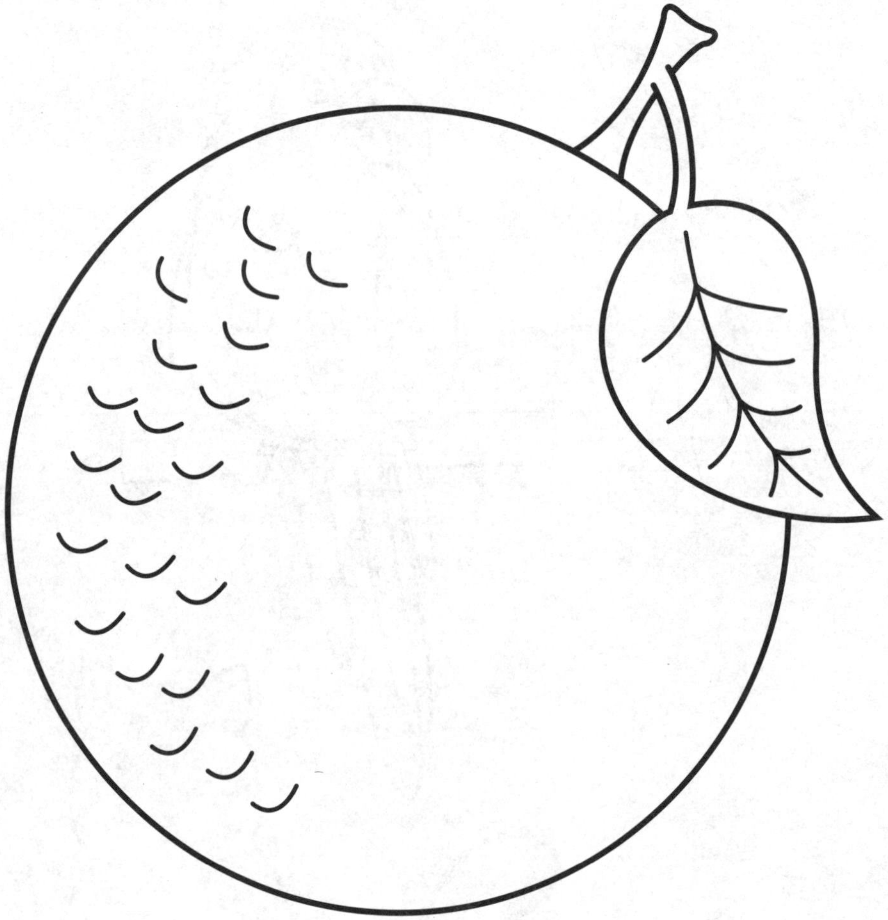

U O

Objectives: Short /o/ and /u/ sounds.

Color and match.

Mathematical Thinking

Learning to Know

8

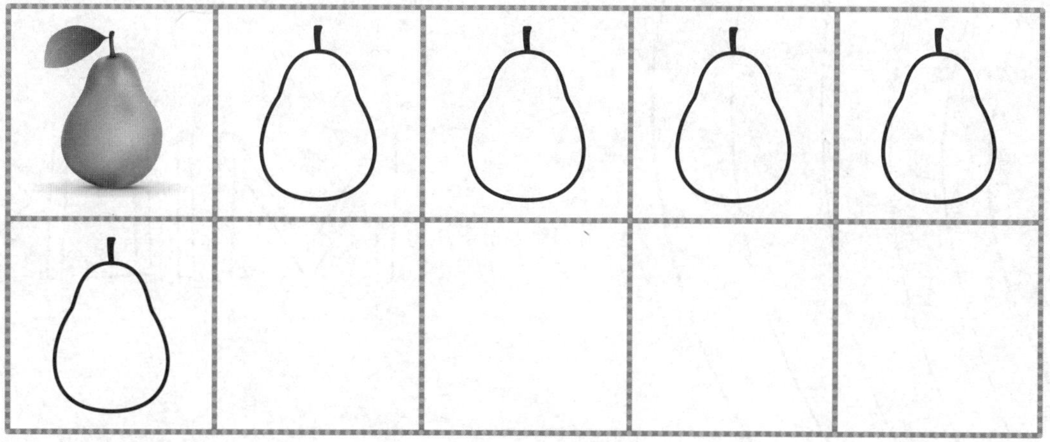

4

6

Objectives: Match numbers with objects to 8.

Developmental Writing

Learning to Know

Trace the shapes.

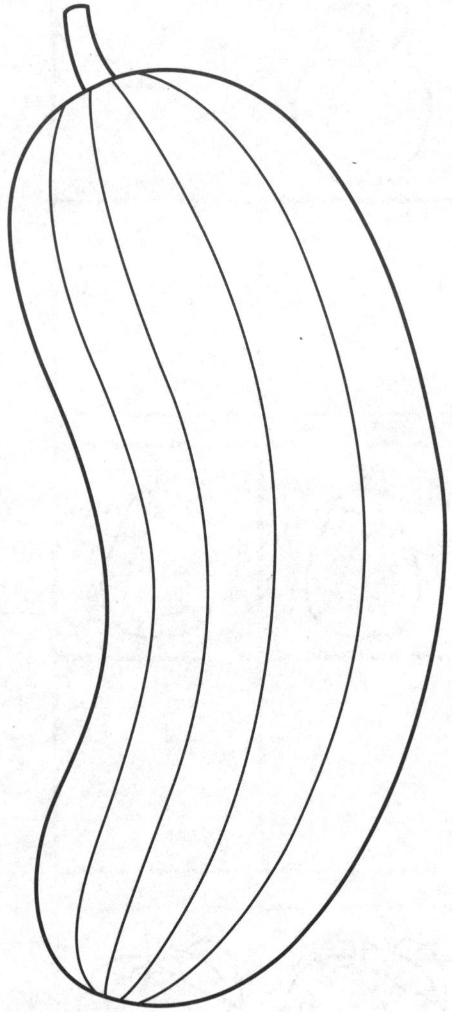

cereal cucumber milk

Color the things you like.

Objectives: Rectangles letter *u*.

Color the fruit with many colors.

Artistic Expression and Appreciation

Learning to Be

Objectives: Food.

Color what you do before you eat.

Physical Development and Health

Learning to Be

Objectives: Personal hygyene.

Phonemic Awareness
Learning to Know

Trace the letters.

u

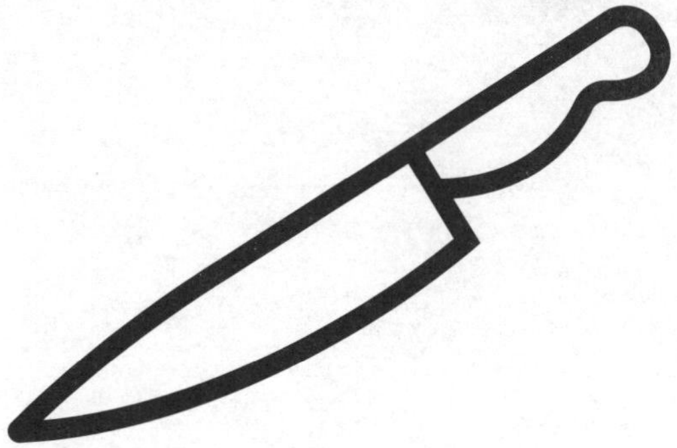

cut

o

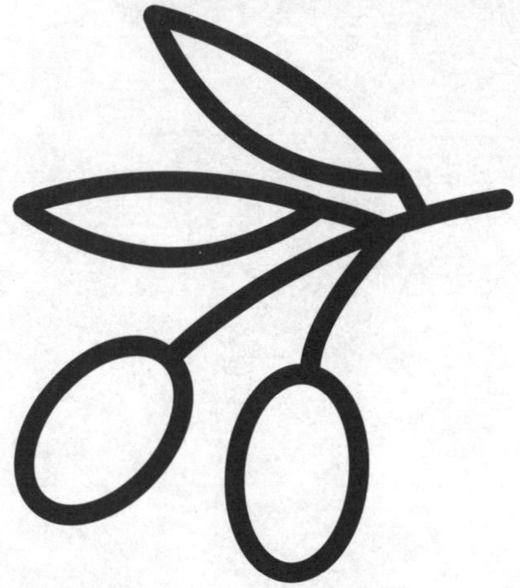

olives

Draw the olives in a salad.

Objectives: Short /o/ and /u/ sounds.

Mathematical Thinking

Learning to Know

Trace the numbers. Draw fruit.

6

7

Objectives: Trace and identify numbers 6 and 7.

Developmental Writing

Learning to Know

Paste string on the oranges. Trace the letters.

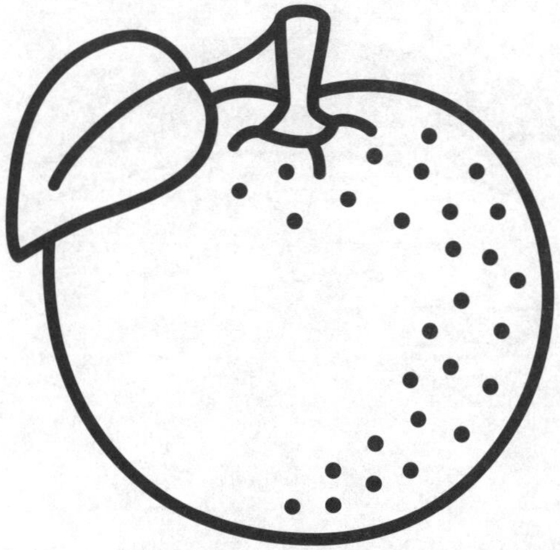

orange

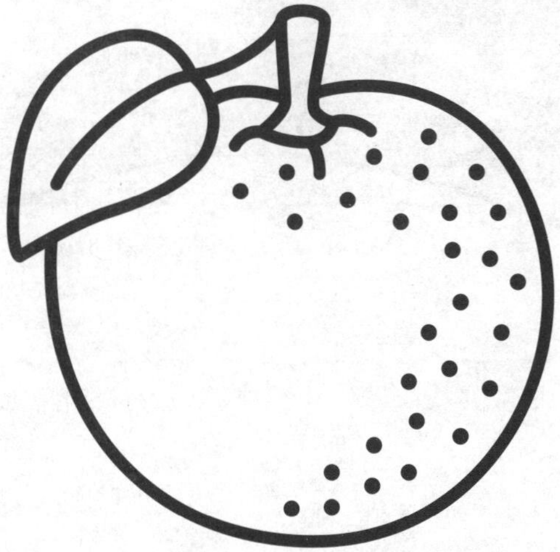

orange

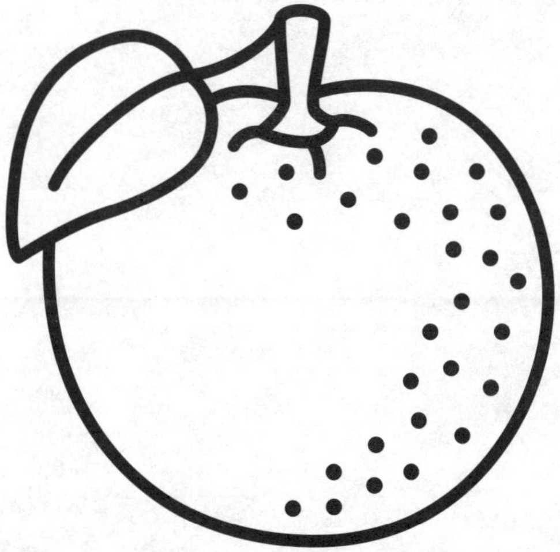

orange

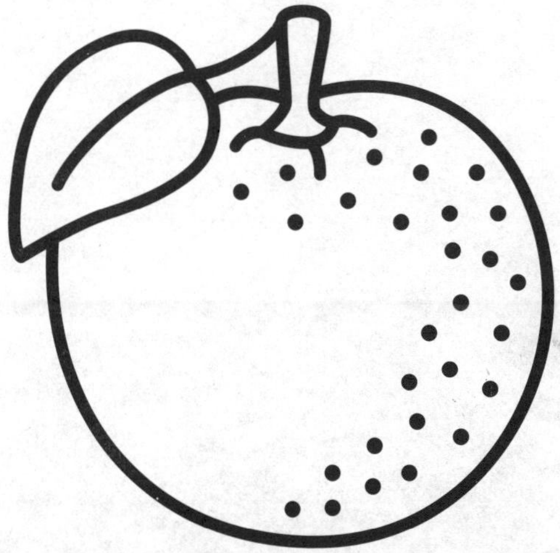

orange

Objectives: Rectangle. Letter *o*.

What do you like in a sandwich? Draw it.

Artistic Expression and Appreciation

Learning to Be

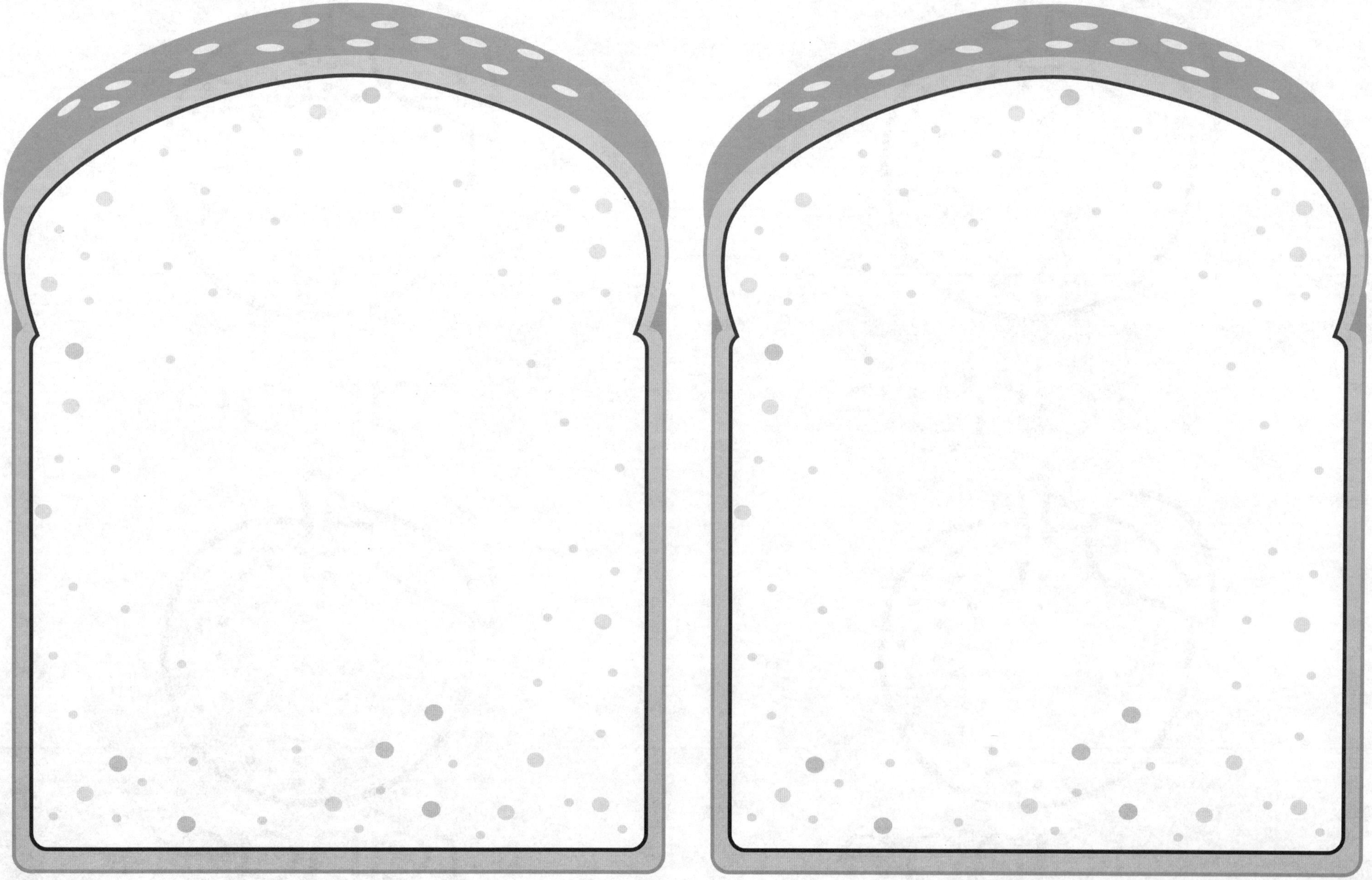

Objectives: Food. Likes and dislikes.

Draw the water you need to clean fruit and vegetables.

Objectives: Hygienic measures with food.

Phonemic Awareness

Learning to Know

Color the things vegetables need to grow.

water and sun

Circle the *u*.

Objectives: Short /o/ and /u/ sounds.

Mathematical Thinking

Learning to Know

Trace the numbers.

8 8 8 8

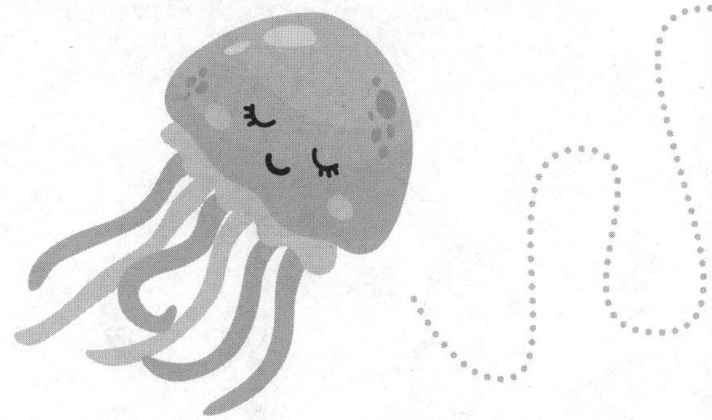

9 9 9 9

0 0 0 0

Objectives: Trace and write 8, 9, and 0.

Developmental Writing

Learning to Know

- **Draw an apple and a carrot where they grow. Trace the *U*.**

up

under

Objectives: Letter *u*.

Find and paste more food in the noodles.

Artistic Expression and Appreciation

Learning to Be

Objectives: Food from other countries.

Draw how you feel after a healthy meal.

Physical Development and Health

Learning to Be

When I eat healthy food, I feel good!

Objectives: Take care of and respect themselves and others.

Circle the correct letter.

o
u

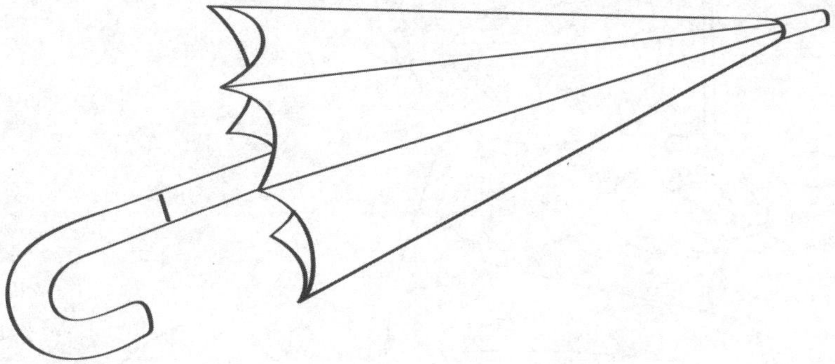

o
u

o
u

o
u

Color the things you don't eat.

Objectives: Short */o/ and /u/* sounds.

Mathematical Thinking

Learning to Know

Match the pictures to the sequence.

First... Next... Then...

Objectives: Sequence simple events.

Developmental Writing

Learning to Know

- **Paste paper on the big letters. Trace the small letters.**

O U

o o o

u u u

- **Trace the shape. Draw and color a fruit that looks like an *o*.**

Objectives: Rectangle. Letter *o*, *u*.

Artistic Expression and Appreciation
Learning to Be

Complete the drawing of a friend.

Objectives: Describe a friend.

Draw food for the baby.

The baby is hungry.

Objectives: Take care of and respect themselves and others.

Color the objects *on* the table purple.
Color the object *under* the table green.

Phonemic Awareness
Learning to Know

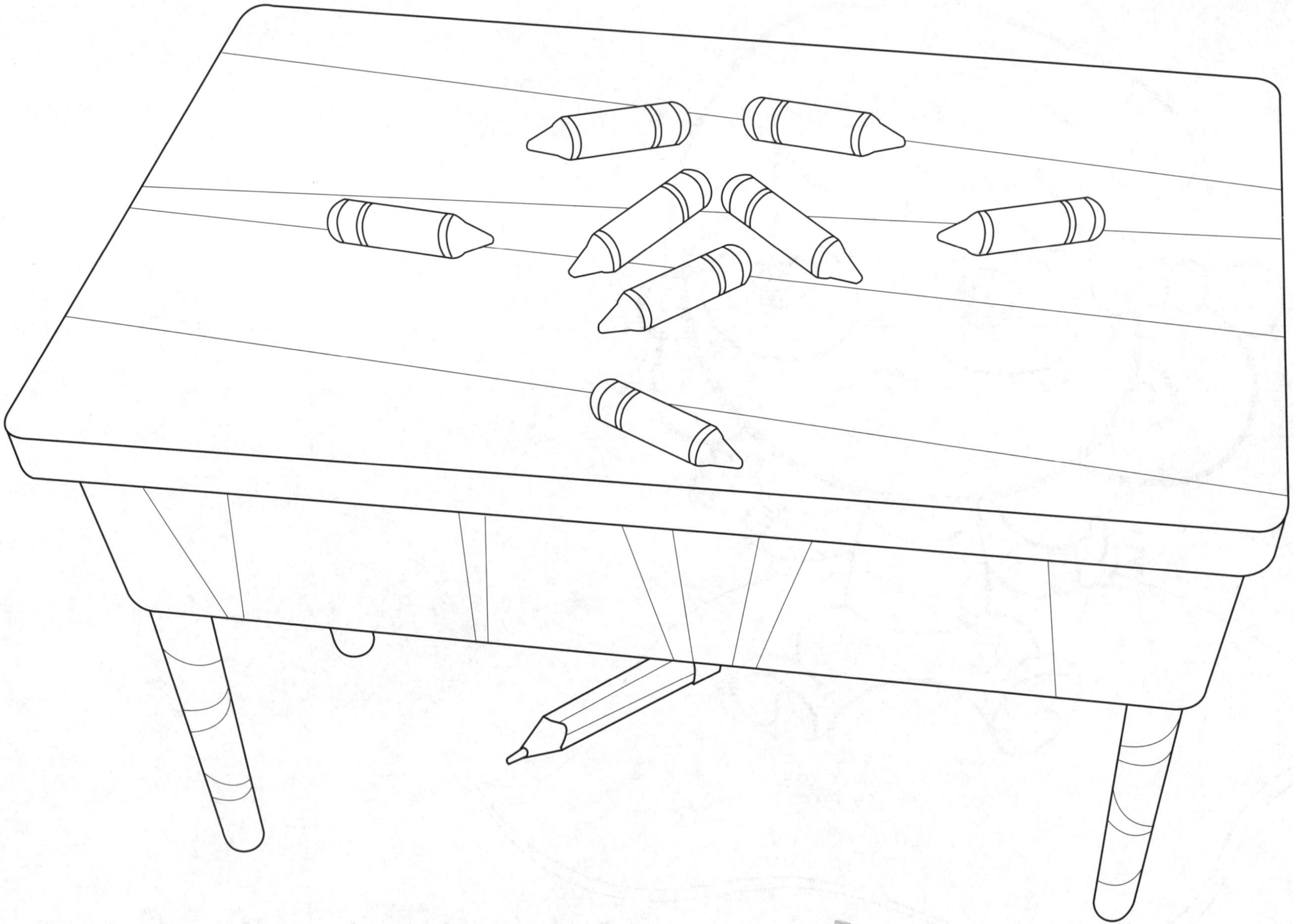

Draw a notebook under the desk.

Objectives: Short /o/ and /u/ sounds.

Extend the pattern.

Mathematical Thinking

Learning to Know

Objectives: Recognize and extend a simple pattern.

Trace the letters with clay.

Developmental Writing

Learning to Know

U u

O o

Objectives: Letters *o*, *u*.

● **Color the object under the table blue and the objects on the table yellow. Circle what is in the box.**

Artistic Expression and Appreciation

Learning to Be

Objectives: Prepositions *in, on, under.*

Match what the children like.

Circle what you like.

Objectives: Recognize that boys and girls can do the same activities.

Phonemic Awareness

Learning to Know

- **Color the umbrella orange, the rug yellow, the otter blue, the bug red.**

Objectives: Short /o/ and /u/ sounds.

Mathematical Thinking

Learning to Know

Match heavy and light food.

Find, cut out and paste one more heavy and light food.

Objectives: Identify heavy and light food.

Developmental Writing

Learning to Know

Trace the letters. Use a different color for *o* and *u*.

u o u o

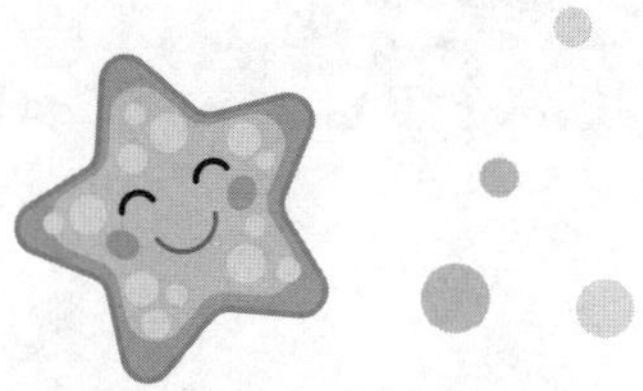

o u o u o u

o u o u o u

Objectives: Letters *o*, *u*.

Artistic Expression and Appreciation

Learning to Be

Cross out what is wrong and check what is correct. ✔ ✘

I write on the chair. ☐ 

I keep my things in my bag. ☐ 

Draw an activity you like at school.

Objectives: School activities.

Color the things you like.

Physical Development and Health

Learning to Be

Objectives: Boys and girls can do the same type of activity.

Phonemic Awareness

Learning to Know

Draw and color a word with an *o* sound and a word with a *u* sound.

Objectives: Short /o/ and /u/ sounds.

Count and write the number. Color.

Mathematical Thinking

Learning to Know

0 1 2 3 4 5 6 7 8 9 10

3 ____

____

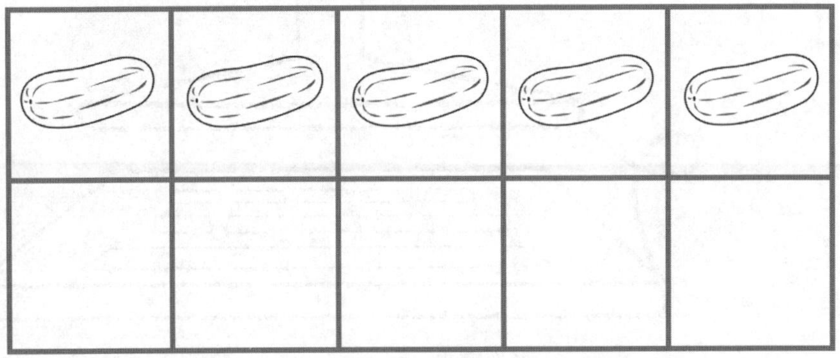

____

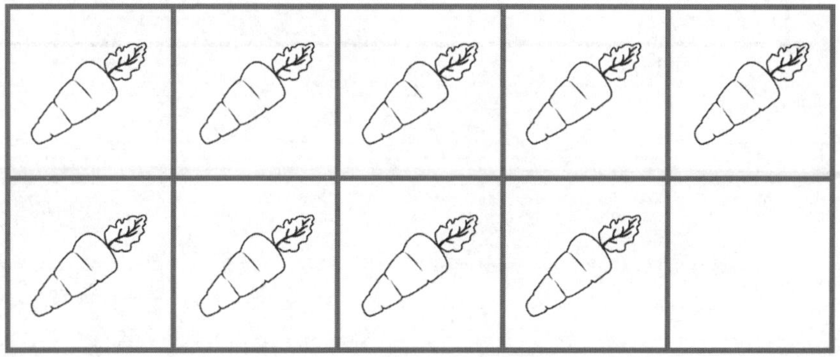

____

Trace the shapes and letters.

Developmental Writing

Learning to Know

school

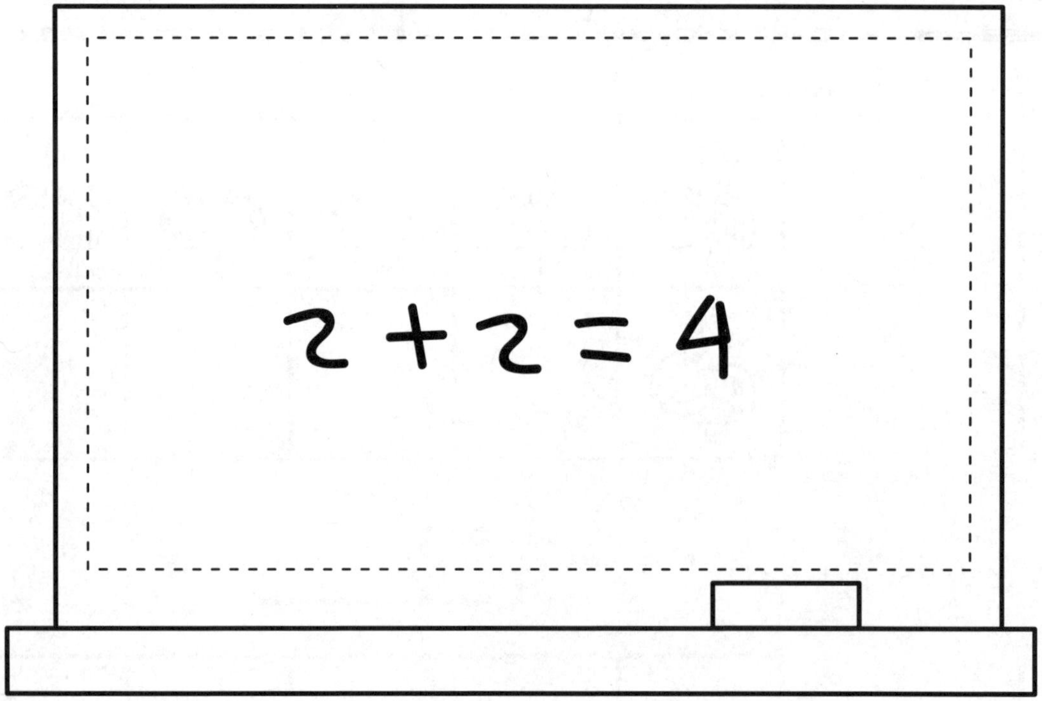

board

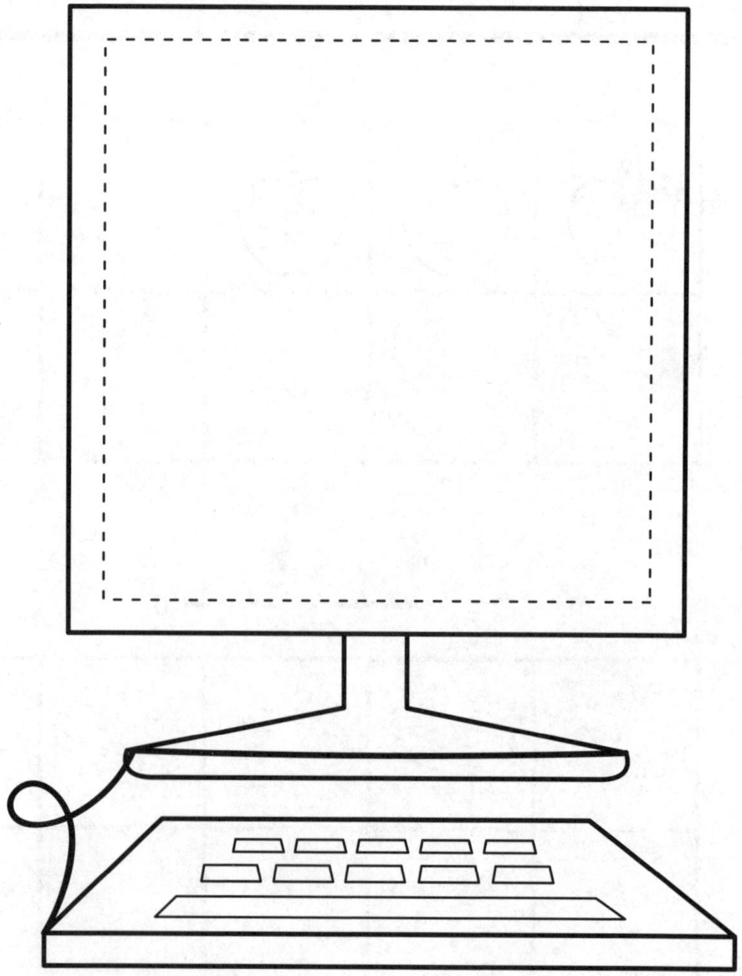

computer

Objectives: Rectangle, square. Letter *o*, *u*.

Use finger paint, crayons, and watercolors.

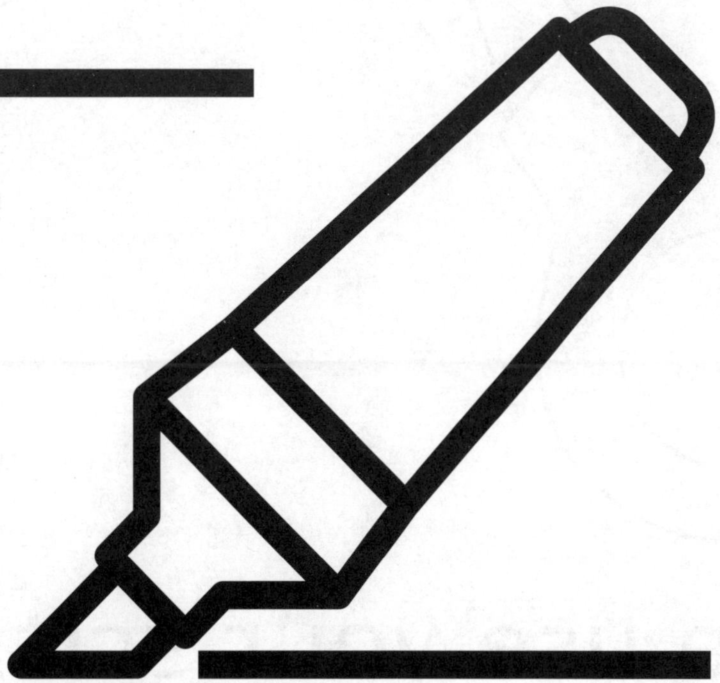

Objectives: Use different techniques to represent objects: finger paint, crayons, watercolors.

- **Use clay to make scissors to give your friend.**

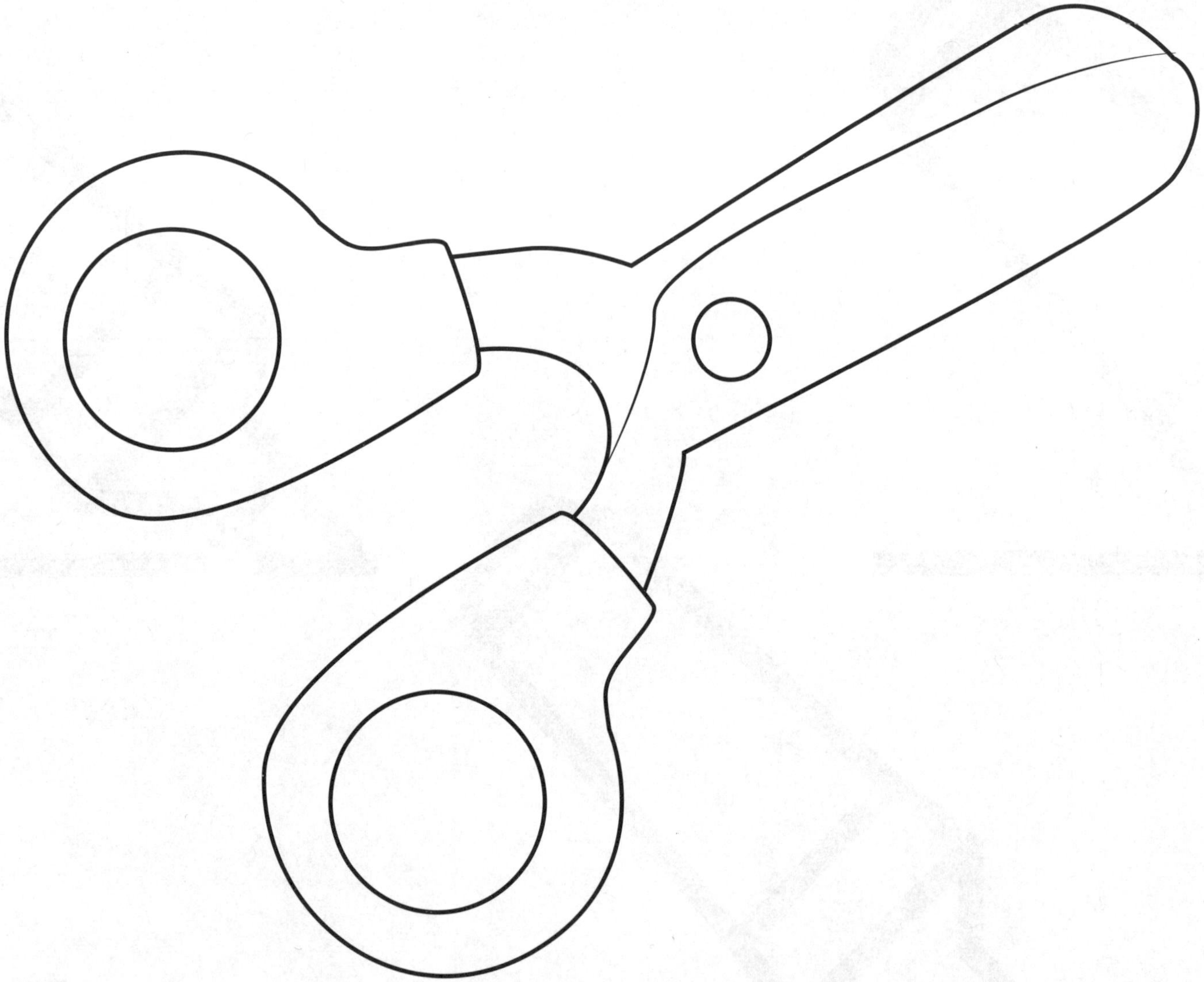

Can I please use your scissors?

Objectives: Be nice to others.

● **Color the things that have a *u*. Circle the *u*.**

Phonemic Awareness

Learning to Know

Uu

sun

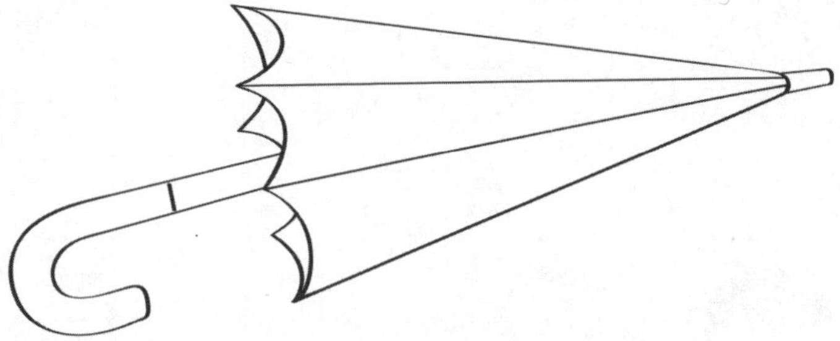

umbrella

puppy

fox

Objectives: Short /o/ and /u/ sounds.

Trace and write the missing the numbers.

Mathematical Thinking

Learning to Know

1 2 3 4 5 6 ___ 8 9 10

1 2 3 ___ 5 6 7 8 ___ 10

1 2 3 4 ___ 6 7 ___ 9 ___

Objectives: Write missing numbers.

Developmental Writing

Learning to Know

Trace and color the letters with finger paint, crayons or watercolors.

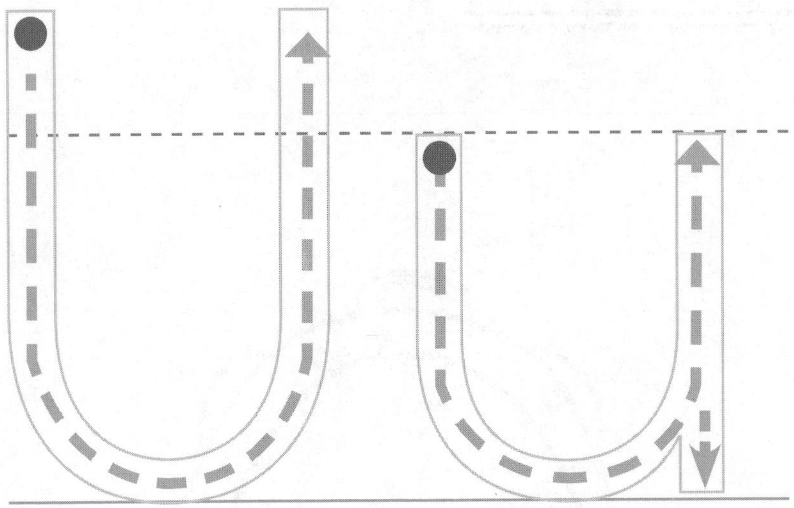

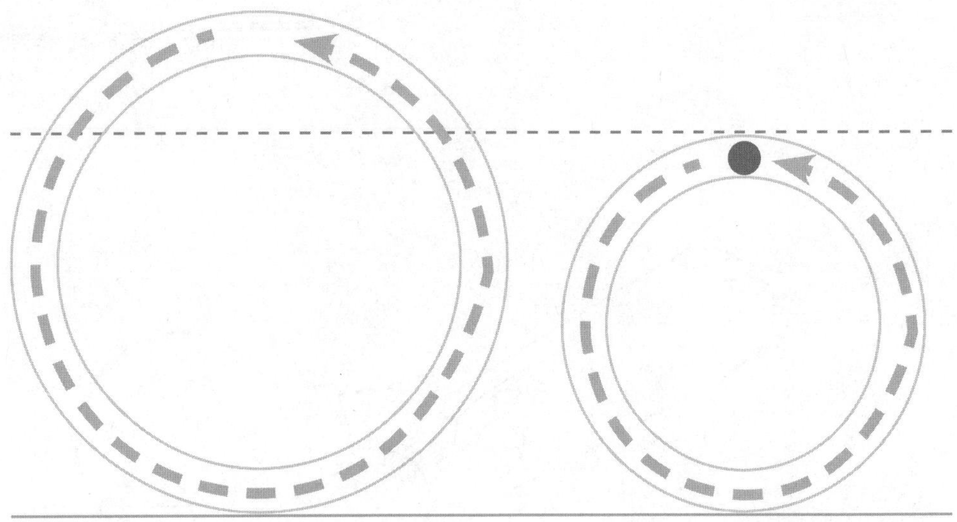

Objectives: Letters *o*, *u*.

Color with finger paint, crayons, and watercolors.

Artistic Expression and Appreciation

Learning to Be

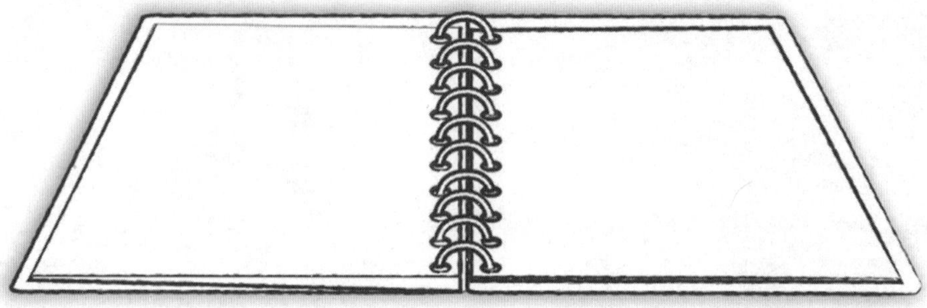

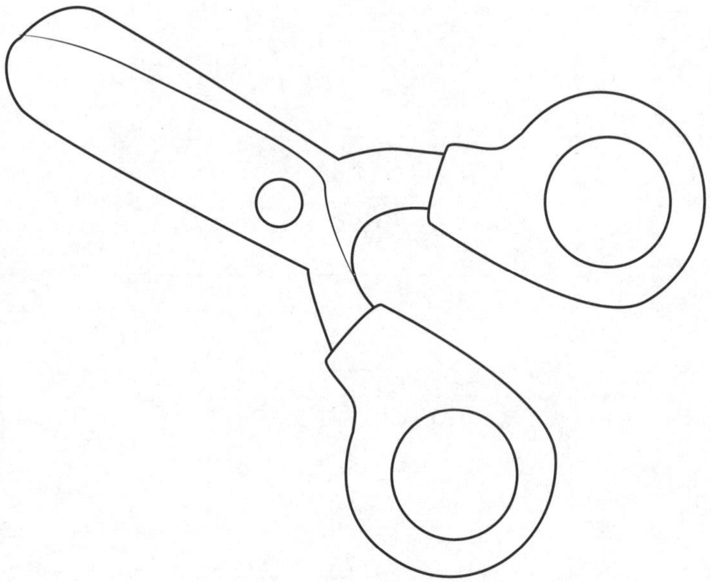

Objectives: Use different techniques to represent objects: finger paint, crayons, watercolors.

Draw two things you like about school.

Personal, Social, and Emotional Development

Learning to Live Together
Learning to Live with Others

We ♥ school!

Objectives: Describe themselves. Likes and dislikes.